CHOOSING JOY

THE SECRET TO LIVING
A FULLY CHRISTIAN LIFE

CHOOSING JOY

THE SECRET TO LIVING A FULLY CHRISTIAN LIFE

Dan Lord

Our Sunday Visitor Publishing Division
Our Sunday Visitor, Inc.
Huntington, Indiana 46750

Dedication

*This book is dedicated to the Holy Spirit,
a Counselor, an Advocate, and
a pure-hearted Friend.*

CONTENTS

ACKNOWLEDGMENTS

I would like to thank Father Paul Zoghby, Father Pat Madden, Dr. Paul Thigpen, Patrick Madrid, Jen and Joe Fulwiler, Sr. Susan (of the Visitation Monastery in Mobile, Alabama), Michael Lord, Jenny Dolan, David Lord, Tony Lord, my dad Chuck, my excellent mom Patricia, Cindy Cavnar for her patience and her amazing editorial guidance, and, finally, Hallie, the most spectacular girl of all time. Thank you all for your wisdom, knowledge, and support.

INTRODUCTION

When you pick up a book that proposes to explore the concept of Christian joy, you expect the author to be an authority. There should be little trifectas of letters after his last name, and perhaps a Roman collar around his neck or a monk's cowl nestled loosely at the back of his head. You should have heard of this guy before or seen him on EWTN. His photo on the dust jacket should imply the joyfulness you're going to learn about in the book.

Instead, it's by me. I've earned no doctorates — I have a Master's in Theology, so that's nice, right? I'm not a priest, but I did seriously think I was being called to be one once, which I strongly suspect is something that real priests secretly make fun of you for. It's like saying to the Navy SEAL: "Yeah, I was going to be a Navy SEAL once. Trained for a couple of weeks to get ready. But, then I decided not to." What is anyone supposed to say to that? It's ultimately just one more thing I almost did but then didn't.

Here's another thing I almost did but didn't: become a famous rocker. I became quasi-famous, I suppose. In the mid-nineties my friend and I started a band, which thousands of millions of young guys do every twenty minutes on average, and we strode confidently down the sidewalk with a bouquet of very sing-able punk rock, horn-driven original tunes for our would-be girlfriend, the World.

And she was pleased. She dated us for a while, and I was head over heels. I loved composing my own songs and hurling them off the edge of a stage and seeing a horde of sweating, subcultural rock enthusiasts devour them. I love music and art and passion and performance. I gave all of that to the World, and in return I enjoyed a level of success: our band had CDs, music videos, a busy touring schedule, a van, a trailer, great fans, mostly-medium-but-also-a-few big-wig music business connections, and the respect of our peers. I was on my way to the top, and the World was pleased with me — as long as I didn't think about anything else.

But you have to think about something else eventually, don't you? There you are on the dance floor with the World, she has her lovely arms around you, the music is playing … but you find that your eyes have started to wander. Your attention drifts when she's in the middle of one of her stories. Your heart just isn't in it anymore. You're falling in love with someone else.

> God had been patiently waiting all that time for his chance to get me momentarily disentangled from the World so he could just talk with me.

At least, that's how I think about it now, and it's with the benefit of hindsight, of course. God had been patiently waiting all that time for his chance to get me momentarily disentangled from the World so he could just talk with me. It was like some religious adaptation of that old Irving Berlin song, "Change Partners," in which the amorous hero, frustrated by the poindexter who's monopolizing his girl's dance card, arranges for the waiter to tell Mr. Third Wheel that he's wanted on the telephone. I guess some similar grace was bestowed on my behalf, helping me take my eyes off the World.

An interior door opened as a result, and God began to just flow right in. That led me to school to be educated in theology and into a whole world of teaching and writing and thinking that had one thing in common: to tell the world that God loves all of us. No, really — that's it. It sounds too saccharine to be true, I'm sure. Or, perhaps, too narrow: "Okay, great, God loves all of us. Is there anything you would like to add?" But, of course, that means there is *everything* to add. Like a book about joy, for instance.

So, here it is.

Now that you have some idea of my peculiar pedigree, I might as well let another cat out of the bag: I am not very good at practicing Christian joy. I see myself, rather, as the equivalent of the overweight sports announcer: he's a passionate fan of the game, he has an understanding of the way it is played to a degree that is maybe a little better than average, but not even by the most strained comparison could he be considered an athlete. He hopes, though, that by his sports announcer-style enthusiasm and his earnest involvement in the subject matter that others will be drawn into a similar love of the game, including (we all hope and pray) a few superior athletes.

Thank you for giving this book a try. God bless.

DAN LORD, 2012

CHAPTER 1

WHAT WE'RE TALKING ABOUT

Joy is not something you would expect to find in someone like my dad.

His father abandoned him and his younger brother when they were both infants. His mother stayed, but she was hard-shelled and aloof. The three of them blew through the slums of 1940's Atlanta like fallen leaves, moving to and from squalid apartments with gaping holes in the walls and broken plumbing. Everyone around them endured the same dreary poverty; one family they knew literally lived in a chicken coop. The males of this world were almost all like my dad's father: human driftwood, coming and going as they pleased, pathetically lazy or darkly savage. My dad once described for me a fight he witnessed between two men which culminated in one of them slicing open the other's stomach with a straight razor. If the hard facts of Chuck Lord's childhood were fed into a big machine that calculated people's fate based on their upbringing, the result would likely read: "Doomed to Joylessness."

Instead, the fatherless boy who lived next to the Chicken Coop family and witnessed the occasional murder has had plenty of joy throughout his life. The primary reason was his conversion to Catholicism.

Virtually nobody he knew as a youth was Catholic — most of them were "holy rollers," as he called them, an ignorant, shallow, unemotional bunch of Flannery O'Connor characters for whom Catholicism may just as well have been Hinduism. He came into the Church circuitously but in relatively short order: at age twenty-three, in fact. Catholicism's elegant logic and transcendent beauty had lured him in, so wonderfully different from the world in which he had grown up.

Sentimentality did not come with the conversion. Perhaps it was his tough upbringing that had kicked into him a certain pragmatism when it came to his faith. A warm-hearted, magnanimous kind of fellow, he nevertheless wasn't the type who looked for signs and wonders from God. For him the Catholic Church was indeed the Pearl of Great Price — he had found it, it was his, and that was enough. He wanted only to serve the truth he had discovered and to be a man worthy of its promises.

Then a miracle happened.

In 1968, thirty-one and happily married, with four kids and a successful career in sales, he strode down Peachtree Street and, on a whim, he let his long legs carry him inside Sacred Heart Catholic Church for a "visit," as he called it — a few minutes of prayer to recollect himself before being carried away by other responsibilities. In the downtown Atlanta of those days you could still do that; the church doors were unlocked from dawn to dusk.

Inside all was serene and quiet. He slipped into a pew near a statue of St. Joseph. Besides his own, the only other movements were the flit of candlelight.

He settled his hard knees onto the soft kneeler and his hands came together in prayer. For a minute or two his mind was a gentle stream, with varying currents of reflective silence or simple, memorized phrases passing through it.

All at once everything changed. The stream was caught up in a sudden tide, an overwhelming feeling that defied explanation. He later used words like "magnificent," "amazing," "warm," "comfortable," and "marvelous," to describe it, but even if you piled them into a wobbling skyscraper of synonyms, they could not come close to describing the actual feeling. He knew that it wasn't the result of a sudden increase of oxygen to his brain or any other merely material cause; it was directly from God, and it was simply awesome in a sense that is infinitely above the way most people use the word *awesome*. He stayed transfixed by it for perhaps forty-five seconds. Then it dissipated.

God had given him a sublime gift: an experience of heavenly joy, unfiltered, as if St. Paul's "dark glass" through which we all see things had been suddenly, temporarily removed. Still in a daze, he thought, "Lord, there may come a day when I will doubt your existence, but I will never forget this." It wasn't a pledge, so much as a statement of simple, unalterable fact which has remained true for all of his life. He has never forgotten it.

There are two reasons this story is important.

First, it reminds us that joy is our ultimate destination. Dad's experience of supernatural joy stands in his memory like a lighthouse, helping to guide him to heaven even on those days when he may be tempted to doubt God's very existence. For those of us who have not had such an experience, we should continually remind ourselves that "the joy of our Master's house" *is the goal.*

Second, it shows that joy as a subject is not only relevant for naïve, untested Doctor Pangloss types who were voted Most Likely To Smile in high school, but for *everybody*, whatever their upbringing or environment, even the people whose lives may have included an extra salvo of kicks to the face.

What It Isn't, What It Is

Ask ten people what joy is and you will get ten different answers: it's pleasure, it's giddiness, it's whatever makes you feel good, it's a brand of dishwasher detergent, it's an Atari game controller if you combine it with *stick,* it's a candy bar if you combine it with *almond.* None of those is right. The best, pithiest definition can be found in a document called *Gaudete in Domino* written by Pope Paul VI in 1975: joy is happiness.

Don't fire up the bumper-sticker machine yet. "Joy is happiness" sounds redundant, for one thing, like "fun is fun." "Happiness" needs a definition, which for Pope

Paul VI was: "peace and satisfaction in the possession of a known and loved good" (7). This peace and satisfaction — joy — comes in degrees, of course, depending on which of the one-hundred-and-twenty-one zillion possible goods you possess. A man smokes an expensive cigar — a small, simple good — and experiences a small, simple peace and satisfaction, a bantamweight joy. Moving up from there into the heavyweight division, where the highest possible degree of joy corresponds to the greatest of all goods, is goodness himself: God.

Of course, experiencing joy isn't *only* a matter of reaching out and grabbing hold of some good. It isn't that simple. If it were, most of us would be deliriously joyful, living in our fully furnished, climate-controlled houses with technological marvels at our beck and call, lavish entertainment, gratifying careers, glazed doughnuts made fresh every morning at the bakery down the street, and so on. It isn't enough; it's *never* enough. That is because, as Pope Paul VI pointed out, "Joy comes from another source. It is spiritual" (9). It is internal. Stack up all the external goods you like, they will never give joy *of themselves*.

The Real Source of Joy

That leads Pope Paul to a reflection on what he refers to as the "secret" of Christian joy, which is, like everything in Christianity, the secret that is meant to be shared with the whole world: the joy of each Christian comes from Jesus Himself. Jesus possesses the highest good possible (God), and he does so perfectly because he *is* God. Each

Person of the Trinity is joy, each fully possesses the other two in perfect, joyful unity. It is Jesus' *essence* to be joyful. The fact that it ends up in us at all is only because he gives it to us.

This is in diametric contrast to what the world tells us about joy. The pervasive creed that lines the seams of our culture like a fungus asserts that joy is something which we provide for ourselves: "*I* give joy to *me*, by acquiring massive sums of material stuff along with a self-gratifying lifestyle that excludes any threat to my narcissistic sense of happiness." If there was ever a time when that way of living, that philosophy, might have seemed justifiable, the past few decades have proven that it is an absolute thumping flop of a failure. Pope Paul VI responds with the melancholic poignancy of a true papa to the plight of the modern souls in his care:

> Money, comfort, hygiene and material security are often not lacking; and yet boredom, depression and sadness unhappily remain the lot of many. These feelings sometimes go as far as anguish and despair, which apparent carefreeness, the frenzies of present good fortune and artificial paradises cannot assuage. (*Gaudete in Domino* 9)

What *can* assuage all of that anguish and despair is Jesus, and only Jesus — Our Lord himself. That isn't a metaphor or a pious bit of religious poetic license. Being a Christian means much more than choosing a particular set of doctrines and moral teachings and faithfully following them — it literally means drawing our life from Jesus. As St. Paul says, "It is no longer I who live, but Christ who lives in me" (Galatians 2:20). We conform everything about us to Our Lord. His joy, therefore, is our joy:

> If you keep my commandments, you will abide in my love, just as I have kept my Father's commandments and abide in his love. These things I have spoken to you, that my joy may be in you, and that your joy may be full. (John 15:10–11)

What's Our Problem, Christians?

A kind of mathematical difficulty may be forming in your mind at this point: roughly one-third of the human race is Christian; more than one billion of them are Catholics, including the sixty-eight-plus million of them who live in the United States. With all of us Christ-followers, shouldn't joy be more readily apparent out there on the landscapes of our world? As a fruit of the Holy Spirit, it doesn't seem to be hanging visibly from a lot of Christian boughs.

… roughly one-third of the human race is Christian; more than one billion of them are Catholics…. With all of us Christ-followers, shouldn't joy be more readily apparent out there on the landscapes of our world?

Therein lie the questions that will concern the remainder of these pages: What is the reason for this absence? Do we consciously exhibit joy? Or are we, maybe, *suppressing* it, putting obstacles in front of it? Is there something we can and should be doing to exhibit this fruit of the Holy Spirit? How do we *know* if we are exhibiting it or not? What does joy "look" like? Are these even questions which should concern us, if this world is indeed a "valley of tears" which we must pass through before attaining the everlasting joy of heaven? Or do we have a *responsibility* to be joyful in this life? My dad was given that snapshot of joy back in 1968 not only so that he could see what lay in store for him if he continued to follow the way of Christ, but also so that he could be familiar with what he ought to be trying to display *now*, in everyday life, no matter the locale.

A Modest Proposal

A discussion of these things is overdue. It has been neglected because it currently occupies a kind of no-man's land between two Christian camps: serious types for whom Christianity is a grave matter with no room for silliness, and silly types for whom Christianity is an emotional matter with no room for seriousness. Not that all Christians belong to one or the other camp, of course — far from it; but the increased tension between the two attitudes has left joy squirming for air like a fish on the beach.

I propose, therefore, a serious discussion of an ecstatic topic since it is, after all, part of the essence of our Christian identities and of our eternal destination. The result, I'm hoping, will be an activation of that which can genuinely transform our sad, angry, anti-life, hard-hearted world: the joy of God.

CHAPTER 2

THE NUTS AND BOLTS OF JOY

Frank Sheed was one of the great twentieth-century Christian apologists. He published best-selling works of theology, and along with his wife, Maisie, he founded the famous Catholic publishing house, Sheed and Ward. He was a top notch scholar and a rock-solid, commonsensical thinker. On top of all that, he had a peculiar habit: he frequently left his London apartment early in the mornings with Maisie so that they could go preach the faith in the public square.

That is very difficult to imagine doing — think of yourself choosing to go down every morning to the mall to start an open discussion about Christianity. Yet it was undeniably effective. One reason is because Frank didn't simply thump a Bible at passersby or issue eschatological warnings. Instead, he presented a public discussion, offering truth in its simple beauty and without threat so that anyone who liked could pause and consider the message of Christ without worrying if there were strings attached.

Some would just listen and move on, others would jeer, but the rusty old wheels of modern man's inner religious apparatus would invariably lurch and turn, at least a little. Conversions followed.

Yet the Frank Sheed of the public square, drawing souls to Christ in his logical, kind-hearted way, was not necessarily the same Frank Sheed who had awakened earlier. Shuffling around the house with creaking limbs, he grumbled about the cold of the English morning, he groused about the futility of his efforts, he wondered aloud why he even bothered with street preaching when nobody ever listened or cared — the kind of low-wattage despair that most every wife has to listen to at one point or another, I suspect.

Regardless, Maisie was always pleased to observe the way that, once the front door was opened and the bright yellow sunlight poured in upon them, Frank transformed. He dropped his complaints and let them clatter to the ground of his mind so that he could be Christ for a Christ-starved world.[1]

The point here is to show that Frank *chose* to display the peace and satisfaction — the joy — that was his as a result of possessing Jesus Christ. It doesn't just automatically emanate from us — we have to choose it; the joy arises from the choosing, in fact.

It shouldn't surprise us that a Christian should have to work at being joyful, unless we are operating under some delusion about the salvation that Jesus offers us, which was never, ever promised to be an instantaneous transfiguration but is, for each man and woman, *a process*. When we say that "Jesus has saved us," we have to mean at the same time that "Jesus is saving us" by a process that, as he clearly demonstrates, includes a lot of anguish, sweat, and pain. Joy is not a flag that Jesus plants in us; it is a fruit that Jesus grows in us.

These Emotions of Ours

Before we look at this image of joy as a *fruit*, some things need to be said about joy as an *emotion*, because it is *that* connotation that tends to dominate our perception.

In Catholic parlance another word for emotions is *passions*. The *Catechism of the Catholic Church* calls joy one of the "principal" passions, along with sadness, fear, desire, and anger. These are gifts from God, although they have no moral value in themselves. They are good or bad depending entirely on how we choose to use them.

Did you catch that? "… on how we choose to use them." As strange as it may seem, emotions are things we are meant to be in charge of — not like Mr. Spock, wrestling to control every emotional surge, but like shepherds, keeping our feelings going down their proper paths. The *Catechism*, quoting St. Thomas Aquinas, goes so far as to state that emotions are *voluntary*, "either because they are commanded by the will or because the will does not place obstacles in their way" (CCC 1767, STh I–II, 24,1 *corp. art.*).

Our Lord shows us what this looks like. He rightly chastises the money-changers in the Temple; his anger completes the act and gives it the proper tone and color. He rightly desires that his people live, and therefore he weeps when Lazarus dies — the sadness shows and confirms the proper aversion to evil (the evil of death). Jesus is God, but he is also the perfect human, therefore his human emotions are expressed perfectly and in harmony with his will.

Because we Christians draw our lives from Jesus — "It is no longer I who live, but Christ who lives in me" (Galatians 2:20) — then of course his emotions are intertwined with ours, and that includes his joy. As we read in the Gospel of John: "If you keep my commandments, you will abide in my love, just as I have kept my Father's commandments and abide in his love. These things I have spoken to you, that my joy may be in you, and that your joy may be full" (John 15:10–11).

Jesus' joy — a vastly fuller, purer joy than any we could cook up on our own — comes as *a result of* keeping his commandments. It is by doing the Lord's will that we experience joy — *doing*, and not just *saying.*

Don't let those words exit your mind without taking note of something that is downright crucial: Jesus' joy — a vastly fuller, purer joy than any we could cook up on our own — comes as *a result of* keeping his commandments. It is by doing the Lord's will that we experience joy — *doing*, and not just *saying.* Let that stand as a sobering reminder to all those who put the emotional cart before the horse of obedience to God. No amount of passionate feelings can ever substitute for God's commandments.

For example, a man may *feel*, with passionate joy, that he is meant to leave his wife for another woman because she's beautiful, sexy, adventurous, and she totally supports his dreams of becoming a winemaker in the south of France. It isn't enough. The commandment of God on this matter, as expressed through the magisterial teaching of the Catholic Church, is incontrovertible and as clear as a warm glass cleaned with Joy brand dish detergent: the commitment made by a man to a woman in a valid, sacramental marriage is an inviolable sacred bond. However difficult it may seem, the man must conform his will to that fact. But in keeping that commandment, Jesus' joy will be his, and that joy will be full and everlasting.

A Fruit of the Holy Spirit

So, now we can move away from talking about joy as an emotion to talking about it as a fruit.

Divine joy is the logical result of faithfully living the life of Christ. It blossoms, like a fruit. That is why St. Paul, in his letter to the Galatians, calls it a fruit of the Holy Spirit. He lists twelve, in fact, though both Augustine and Aquinas assure us that it is not meant to be a complete list[2]: charity, joy, peace, patience, kindness, goodness, generosity, gentleness, faithfulness, modesty, self-control, and chastity. They all come about as a result of 1) having the Holy Spirit within you and 2) living in harmony with God's will.

This involves a very purposeful, very personal "yes" from you to him, every day, and every single minute of every day. But it isn't just *that* — it isn't just a matter of holding on to the hand of the Creator and letting him lead you. It means becoming mystically one with Jesus and drawing our life from him. "Apart from me you can do nothing," he says (John 15:5), but through him, with him, and in him, our "yes" to God becomes more than just a temporary choice — it becomes our defining feature.

What Do Sacraments Have to Do With It?

To enable us to say the *yes* now that will, by God's mercy, translate into eternity, God gives us himself in the sacraments of Baptism and Confirmation (and the Eucharist, too, which we'll discuss later). They go together in a little group the Church calls the Sacraments of Initiation and, frankly, in a world that has lost its sense of the sacramental, they could use some good press.

Baptism, if you didn't know it, is mind-bogglingly awesome. Sadly, it has been forgotten by the world and reduced to a simple social ritual that is used primarily to say: "Look! A new baby! We the parents are going to really take care of him and teach him about Jesus. Now, let's go eat some cake."

Suffering a roughly similar fate, the sacrament of Confirmation is often perceived as little more than a coming-of-age ceremony. For whatever reason, the average Catholic can never seem to find the words to explain or even describe Confirmation, that ultrapowerful explosion of the grace that was given to us in Baptism.

To appreciate the effects of these two sacraments, it might help to picture them this way: *Baptism* takes a twisted broken vessel (you or me, born into the badly broken human race) and remakes it into the shape of the Holy Spirit and then fills it with grace, the life of God. *Confirmation* gives that new creature the power to suddenly spring up and become an action hero fighting for the Kingdom of God. To live out our *full* Christian lives here on earth, it is not enough to be baptized — the New Testament tells us that (see, for instance, Acts 8:14–17). Confirmation is meant to unleash what has been waiting in you since you were a baby hovering over the baptismal font with your family gathered around you.

The gifts that we receive when we are confirmed are: understanding, counsel, fortitude, piety, fear of the Lord, knowledge, and wisdom. These are not human gifts. Each of them is calibrated to receive power from God himself. As the baptized-and-confirmed Christian goes through life using these gifts, he or she becomes more and more one with them, more proficient, more at ease with them — like a professional boxer. After training for weeks under a wise guide, a pro boxer knows exactly what to do with his fists and with his legs. He knows how to keep his guard up and how to strike when the time is right. His very breathing is an art and a science. The gifts given him by his trainer are not just attachments or accoutrements, but have become essential to the boxer. In the same way, the gifts that the Holy Spirit gives to baptized-and-confirmed men and women also become more and more part of them as they practice them and use them in the daily struggle of Christian living.

Father Edward Leen once described the whole thing this way: "When the action of the gifts becomes more constant in the life of the Christian, the infused virtues take more perfect hold of the intellect and will…,"[3] which all happens *only* if there is a "sustained docility to the Holy Spirit dwelling within."[4]

The stupendous result is (by metaphor) fruit: the fruits of the Holy Spirit, as they are known.

A Tree with a Mind

The Bible occasionally compares us to trees that God has planted, and we are indeed the weirdest of trees because we don't simply react to the Gardener's efforts — we co-operate with them. Every day he comes out to water us, and we say "yes." We lift our branches and say, "A little extra over here, please," even though he already knows that. We can say "no", as well: "I don't want or need your water. I can take care of myself." That's a stupid thing to do, of course. We should let him water us; doing so is an example of that docility that Father Leen is referring to — and by docility he doesn't mean being passive, just sitting there like a lump and letting God do everything while we consciously do nothing. St. Thomas Aquinas, who wrote so much about the fruits of the Holy Spirit, was, in fact, physically shaped like a giant lump, but that isn't how he acted. He lived his love for God with all his heart, all his soul, and all his mind in the way his thoughts always remained fixed on the divine, to the point that when relatives one day offered him sex with a prostitute, he flew into a rage, shouting and waving them all away as if they were a colony of bats. *That* is being docile to the Holy Spirit dwelling in your soul.

So, the Tree with a Mind grows every day, nourished and watered by the Gardener. The roots extend farther into the ground; the bark becomes strong enough to block bullets; the branches reach out and are so thick with broad green leaves that it provides a shade to smaller, weaker trees growing alongside it. And, when the season comes, at exactly the perfect time, fruit grows.

Fruit is what the Gardener has been waiting for. The tree reaches its perfect maturity, its fulfillment, when the fruit blossoms. Now it's harvest time. The fruits, for the Christian, are things like joy. Joy is what happens as the result of choosing God, being baptized and confirmed in the Holy Spirit, following the commandments of Jesus Christ and serving him, training every day with the gifts of the Spirit and putting them into action. All of this grows the tree, and the tree bears fruit: charity, joy, peace, patience, kindness, and all the others.

The thing about this kind of fruit is: it grows even when the weather turns bad. Even if everything around you becomes a wasteland, a Mordor, you are the strong tree bearing fruit. This is why Jesus can dare to stand up and tell us that the poor in spirit are blessed, as well as the meek and mournful. The Beatitudes are completely preposterous otherwise. *The meek are not blessed,* says the world. *They are trampled and taken advantage of and mocked. The poor are not blessed — they're poor. They have nothing! They don't have enough to feed their own children properly and their cars are broken down and they can't get a job! These are not blessings!*

But for God's boxer who has trained, who has assimilated the gifts of his Trainer, for God's stout tree that has cooperated with the Great Gardener, the fruits burst forth even when everything around you is what ungodly people can only call a curse. Afflictions lose their power against you, because you have become "a little Christ," who was crucified; it is he who lives in you.

A Prelude to Obstacles

So, what stands in our way? What, really, prevents us from being joyful?

Dr. Peter Kreeft once wrote that each of us has two enemies, and only two. He gives a long list of people we might assume are our enemies that in actuality are not: heretics, bigots, media figures in the service of the culture of death, and so forth. Really, our two enemies are evil spirits and us.[5]

Of the two, the worst, Dr. Kreeft assures us, is ourselves. Now let's take a good, honest look at the obstacles we place between us and the gifts God gives us.

CHAPTER 3

WELCOME HOME, MISERABLE SELF-LOATHERS: OBSTACLE ONE

When you try to imagine a Self-Loather, what might come to mind is a potbellied sad sack standing off in a corner, rummaging through the dirt with his left foot and wondering why God ever made him.

The truth is that sometimes the most industrious guy in the group is the one who cannot stand himself. That's why he's moving so fast, doing so much, working so hard to earn approval, perhaps even to the point of seeming like he's arrogant or condescending. The secret is: he loathes himself.

Maybe that person is you. Whatever perception people have of you, either as a sad sack or a captain of industry or something else, to lug around a persistent negative self-image is a Sisyphean agony and a rot upon the fruit of joy that Gods wants to grow in you. Self-loathing has many roots, of course, and careful counseling can help a self-loather figure out where he got stuck and how he can change. Our human inclination to sin lies behind much of it, along with our tendency to sink beneath sin's weight. For a vast number of people it is this sin-related self-loathing that is an obstacle to joy.

> Whatever perception people have of you, either as a sad sack or a captain of industry or something else, to lug around a persistent negative self-image is a Sisyphean agony and a rot upon the fruit of joy that Gods wants to grow in you.

If you are among them (and I think most of us are at some point), take some comfort in the fact that you are descended from a long line of Self-Loathers, starting with Adam and Eve. Recall how, after their heinous sin against God (which, just to be clear, was *not* eating a magic, organically grown apple, but literally trying to usurp the power and authority of God)[6] they hid themselves away. They were right to feel ashamed, but they were not right to assume that their relationship with God was now one of enmity. God did not hate them. The thing about sin, particularly mortal sin, is that it is so utterly destructive that after it's done, we can tend to think that it defines us. There is nothing else to us, we assume — we *are* sin, and therefore God can't possibly love us.

God cannot grow fruit in a person who refuses to allow him to do so, but because he is a Father, he continues to love that person. God the Father, who is Love, loves his children ... even when they hate themselves. When they assume he wants nothing to do with them and they hide themselves away, he is close, as he was with Adam and Eve.

No, they can't stay in Paradise, of course, because Paradise was designed for people who are sinless, just like cars are designed for people who are competent drivers. You would no more leave a Paradise under the care of broken, sinful people then you would leave a shiny new Aston Martin in the hands of a werewolf — the result would be chaos all around. So, Adam and Eve had to go; but note the little detail Genesis gives us as they are on their way out. God the Father does the most intimate, loving, fatherly thing in the world for them — even motherly, when you get right down to it: he makes some clothes for them (Genesis 3:21).

Wearing the Clothes That God Gave You

You are not your sin. You are a child of God. He never stops loving you, and he continues to provide "clothes" for you — i.e., all the things you need to keep progressing in your relationship with him. Ergo, stop hating yourself. To really confront this problem will necessitate some quiet reflection; if possible, some good pastoral guidance; most definitely a trip to the confessional. Self-loathing will forever prevent the Holy Spirit from producing joy in you unless you do something about it.

Proper Handling and Care of Sins

Oh, great, you might be thinking with an irritated sigh, *so it's back to sin, the Catholic Church's favorite subject.* It isn't the Church's favorite subject; everlasting joy in heaven is. But a discussion of joy absolutely must include a healthy discussion of the reality of sin and how it should be dealt with.

Guilt is a gift. It is an internal alarm system meant to help guide us away from sin: "For the man who has committed evil, the verdict of his conscience remains a pledge of conversion and of hope" (CCC 1797). It is true whether you call yourself Christian or not — we all have some concept of an objective moral law, and whenever we observe a violation of some aspect of it, we all hear the whine of the guilt alarm. Simply abandoning traditional Christianity, as so many have done in recent decades, does not remove the alarm. All we've done is throw away the instruction manual for what to do when the alarm goes off. When it does, our reactions will vary. For instance:

1. Pretend it isn't going off, although the sound will probably drive you nuts in time.
2. Seek material distractions; take an "I'm too busy having fun to feel guilt" attitude. Prepare for early hair loss, high blood pressure, and a steady transformation into a Self-Loather.
3. Choose a religion, preferably something syncretistic and "non-denom," something that doesn't make you acknowledge too much guilt, some-

thing nice — anything but Catholicism, because we all know how *those* people are.

The common fact that each of these reactions denies to one degree or another is this: we are moral actors in God's universe. We are wired to want to know the truth even when we've lost hope of finding it. We want to know how to act, and we all have a conscience that helps us to act. Denying all that, suppressing it, or refusing to apply our will and intellect appropriately only leaves the entire system in the hands of our lower nature: our instincts, our impulses, reactions stamped onto us by parents and siblings and followed blindly; yes, even the promptings of evil spirits. These are all monkeys left in charge of your ship. You'll be driven all over the place by them, into all kinds of obsessive behaviors, bad habits, and superstitions, a whole noisy gamut of scrupulous fidgeting, and only because, paradoxically, we left behind the traditional Christianity that we thought was so scrupulous.

The answer is to come back to the Church. The Holy Spirit not only expresses heavenly commandments through her, but gives her people the capacity to receive them properly so that "the law of the LORD is their joy" (Psalm 1:2, NAB).

The Unconsidered Factor

Some time ago I showed up for a meeting with a priest to talk about some serious spiritual struggles I was going through. Not just "going through," actually, but "had been going through for years."

My wife knew all about them. She'd had many a night's sleep interrupted because her crazy husband woke up throwing punches at things that nobody saw but him. Huge spiders would open like black umbrellas on the ceiling, or terrible amorphous shapes would hover near my face. You may have heard of the phenomenon of dark figures standing in the corners of rooms watching people — one of those people being watched was *me*. Behaviorally, I was mercurial and volatile, easily swept up by frenzied losses of temper or wild impulses that tore me away from things I needed to be doing.

At the same time, I wanted to be the undisputed Best Dad and Husband Ever. I was keenly aware of God's generosity in bringing me back into the Catholic Church and giving me an excellent wife and precious children, and I wanted to treat his gifts with the utmost care and love. But that wasn't happening. I was too temperamental; I was *weird*. Weirdness works when you're the frontman for a traveling rock band as I was a long time ago; it doesn't work when your wife just wants you to go to sleep and stop yelling at the Demon Man at the foot of the bed.

What does any of this have to do with self-loathing? The priest I went to meet that day spotted my self-loathing from a mile off. I denied it: *I don't hate myself. I'm tough. I'm confident.* Yes, I admitted to him, there have been all kinds of awful things I've done to myself and to other people throughout my life, but I'd gone to Confession for those things. I continue going to Confession in response to new sins — I *like* going to Confession; I know it heals me.

What the priest was able to do, however, by a slow, patient process of prayer and dialogue, was identify two facts about me.

One was that I thought of myself as indistinguishable from the sins I had committed in life. The Church doesn't teach that; I made that up on my own in some dismal subconscious cavern. It was that very priest, in fact, who taught me the line I used on you earlier in this chapter: "You are not your sin." I'm a baptized child of God, essentially good, sometimes broken due to sin, but always within reach of a loving Father who just wants to clean his child up and see him walk like a man.

The second thing the priest identified about me was that I had several times over the course of my life made myself available to actual evil spirits. They were still with me — demons, I mean. No, not pop psychology demons, not memories of traumatic experiences, but *demons*. It's alright to laugh — many aspects of the experience have often struck me as funny, too.

All jokes aside, it is evil spirits that are the "unconsidered factor" alluded to at the beginning of this section. I always like to emphasize that I never consciously invited the damned things in — but I lived in such a way that it left me wide open. Therein lies what might be a helpful metaphor, in fact: in a big city, if you keep your doors locked and take other commonsense precautions, you will be less likely to have your apartment broken into. On the other hand, if you always leave your door open, leave your belongings unprotected, and brag loudly on your stoop about how you couldn't care less about someone breaking in, then it won't be long before you'll fin your apartment occupied by unsavory fellows. So it is with your spiritual apartment; I'd been a fool with mine, and now I had some dastardly residents who refused to exit. By the cleansing power of Jesus, the priest rid me of those residents.

I bring all of this up *just in case* you might be wrestling with some strangely persistent vice like my self-loathing that won't go away no matter how many novenas you pray, blocking the way between you and the full, joyful life God has in mind for you. The problem *might* have something to do with evil spirits. I'm not the only dummy to live his life without proper reference to an objective moral law, so I doubt I'm the only guy who has had to suffer the inevitable spiritual consequences. In fact, at this point, I know it beyond a doubt. If you suspect you might be in the same boat I was, see a priest.

And don't make the mistake of thinking: "Well, I'm not tied up in my room howling like a wolf and spewing profanity in strange, foreign languages. I get up and go to work like everybody else, and I love Jesus. I'm fine, right?" As Tom Hoopes once wrote: "… the truth is, the victims of demonic activity don't live in carnival haunted houses. They exist at the edges of a malaise. They're anxious or depressed, disoriented in their spiritual lives or slowly losing their minds — always wondering if the thoughts filling their heads are really their own."[7]

If this is all starting to jangle some warning bells for you, then: 1. Pray to the Holy Spirit for guidance; 2. Talk to a priest (though finding one who will take you seriously could prove challenging); and 3. See it through to the end — don't begin the investigation and then let it be overwhelmed by the ordinary goings-on of life.

But don't rule it out just because it has become popular to rule it out. The Church still carries on the mission of Christ, which has not changed for two thousand years: "to destroy the works of the devil" (1 John 3:8). Believers in Jesus are known by the fact that, among other things, they "cast out demons" (Mark 16:17).

CHAPTER 4

PEACE VS. ANXIETY: OBSTACLE TWO

At Mass, at the conclusion of the Our Father, the priest makes a special request of God: "Protect us from all anxiety as we wait in joyful hope…." Following the Lord's Prayer, the priest recalls the words of Jesus: "I leave you peace, my peace I give you." So, within a very short span we ask God to dispel anxiety and are reminded of the exact opposite of anxiety: the gift of peace.

Peace is third on St. Paul's list of fruits, right after charity and joy. In fact, in Galatians the Greek word for *fruits* is actually rendered in the singular, perhaps implying that the fruits of the Holy Spirit ought to be considered as one, a kind of "seamless garment" of fruits.

St. Thomas Aquinas explains that the order of fruits as they are listed is not an accident, either.[8] Charity must be first, of course — love, because "God is love, and he who abides in love abides in God, and God abides in him" (1 John 4:16). Love is the water in which we Christian fish exist. If we don't have *that*, we can have shimmering, opalescent scales and powerful fins that propel us at terrific speeds, we can have preternatural gifts of sonar detection and glow-in-the-dark appendages, but if we don't have water then we're just dead, dried, fish meat.

So, charity or love is the logical first fruit of the Holy Spirit that is listed in Galatians. The second one, joy, is what St. Thomas calls charity's "sequel." It follows necessarily: to suddenly have real love, and no less than the personal love of God himself, is to be filled with unutterable joy. Then comes what Aquinas calls "the perfection" of joy, what happens when the true joy of God is ours: peace, the third fruit listed in Galatians. "I leave you peace," says Jesus in the liturgy, "My peace [the everlasting peace of God that is the essence of God's nature] I give you."

That peace is two-fold, Aquinas explains. One: it is "freedom from outward disturbance." Two: peace is "the calm of restless desire;" meaning that the desire which has always moved our hearts toward our Lord in heaven is at last completely satisfied. That's a peace that surpasses all understanding (see Philippians 4), and yet it's ours. It is our heritage, as baptized Christians.

The Dark-Helmeted Archenemy of Peace

Then why are we so anxious all the time? There was a very good reason that Blessed John Paul began his pontificate in 1979 with the words "Be not afraid." The reason was: because we desperately needed to hear it. No doubt the Christian citizens of the moribund Roman Empire in the fifth century were anxious about the Visigoths hammering against the gates; certainly the bubonic plague of the 1300s caused people plenty of knee-quaking anxiety, but I will dare guess that there has been no society in all the societies since the Ascension that was as anxious as our own. Anxiety is the air we breathe; it lives and grows in us the way that mold grows in the walls of damp houses. We are worried about absolutely, positively *everything*.

> Anxiety is the dark-helmeted archenemy of peace. Its presence in our hearts betrays an absence of the peace of God. If we don't fend it off, it worms into all the fruits of the Holy Spirit that have been given to us, including joy.

Anxiety is the dark-helmeted archenemy of peace. Its presence in our hearts betrays an absence of the peace of God. If we don't fend it off, it worms into all the fruits of the Holy Spirit that have been given to us, including joy. Anxiety, therefore, is an obstacle to joy.

Martha and Mary

"Do not be anxious about tomorrow," we read in the Gospel of Matthew (6:34). That immediately makes sense to us. We read that, and it goes directly to our hearts — we know that here Jesus is telling us things that are true and vital, even if difficult to put into practice. Yet even the most earnest, well-intentioned folk will be snared by anxiety.

As with Self-Loathers, they're in good company — namely, Jesus' good friends, the sisters Martha and Mary. There is a beloved and well-known story about them in the Gospel of Luke. The strange thing about this story is that it is not only about the pitfalls of anxiety, but it also seems to be a Luciferian favorite for leading people subtly into confusion about what Jesus expects of us.

If there is truth to that latter observation, it shouldn't completely surprise us. "Mark you this, Bassanio," says Antonio in *The Merchant of Venice*, "The devil can cite Scripture for his purpose." Shakespeare was clearly familiar with the fourth chapter of Matthew's Gospel in which Satan leads Jesus into the desert to tempt him using, of all things, Psalm 91, which is unambiguously about putting all of one's trust in God! Since we, as Jesus' followers, can expect similar scriptural tomfoolery, it is a good idea to take a closer look at the Martha and Mary story so that we can ascertain what the Holy Spirit is trying to say with it:

> Now as they went on their way, [Jesus] entered a village; and a woman named Martha received him into her house. And she had a sister called Mary, who sat at the Lord's feet and listened to his teaching. But Martha was distracted with much serving; and she went to him and said, "Lord, do you not care that my sister has left me to serve alone? Tell her then to help me." But the Lord answered her, "Martha, Martha, you are anxious and troubled about many things; one thing is needful. Mary has chosen the

good portion, which shall not be taken away from her." (Luke 10:38–42)

Here's how some modern readers explain this story to themselves: Martha is a naturally industrious, hard-working kind of girl. She would like to sit and listen to Jesus, but there's just no time, and there are things that absolutely need to get done. Mary, on the other hand, is a naturally reflective, brainy kind of person. She could help Martha with the things around the house, but she chooses to neglect those tasks in favor of listening to Jesus.

On that reading, it is natural for many people to have a reaction sort of like this: "Welllll, of *course* I admire Mary for stopping everything to listen to Jesus, and that *is* the right thing to do, but … but … isn't the story kind of unfair to Martha who was, after all, just doing her job? All the stuff needing to be done in the house really needs to be done! *Somebody* has to do it! In fact, the Bible and the Church make it consistently clear that we are to fulfill our responsibilities in life, to live out our vocation. St. Padre Pio himself said 'duty first, even before something holy.' So, why does Martha get chewed out by the Lord and Mary get a pat on the back?"

Not wishing to criticize the wisdom of God, however, people then proceed, very often, to build an entire anthropology based on this interpretation. God, they decide, must have created two kinds of people: Marthas and Marys. Marthas are industrious, fastidious, and straight-forward; they do not like to sit still, they like to stay busy and get things done. Marys, on the other hand, like to read long books about praying, and they build shrines in their closets and look for occasions to daydream about what heaven will be like. More than once I've heard someone exclaim, either in conversation or in a combox: "I just can't do novenas — I'm a Martha! I have to stay busy, sweep the floor, organize the tool shed — but isn't that an act of praise, in its own way, after all?"

This entire strained Martha/Mary philosophy, we should all be glad to discover, is unnecessary because it derives from a misunderstanding of the story.

St. Francis de Sales provides the clarity we need. His *Introduction to the Devout Life* is a masterpiece, filled from cover to cover with practical advice and wisdom on how to live out our lives as Christians.

St. Francis points out that Jesus does not admonish Martha for working hard, or for doing her job. He admonishes her *because she goes about her work anxiously*: "Martha, Martha, you are anxious and troubled about many things."

"Note," writes St. Francis, "that she would not have been troubled if she had been merely diligent, but she was over-concerned and therefore hurried about and troubled herself. It was for this reason that our Lord rebuked her."[9]

This interpretation gets away from fixating on Martha and Mary as Personality Camps to one or the other of which each of us must belong. Using St. Francis as a guide, we can see that the point of the story is to not let anxiety stick its nose in our business. There is a huge challenge here, by extension, for all of us. How can we work at our jobs, make breakfast for our kids, pick up some faucet parts om the hardware store, fix a flat tire, fold the laundry, cut the grass, teach our six-year-old how to subtract, teach our fifteen-year-old how to drive, teach our twenty-year-old why it isn't wise to date forty-year-olds, and pay our bills without being *anxious* about any of it? We're called to be careful in our work (just like Martha) and diligent (just like Martha), but totally reliant on Jesus and trusting in him, always "listening" to him (like Mary).

What this also means is that, suddenly, every single thing we do in life, from swabbing baby bottoms to filing our taxes, becomes a theater where drama of the most profound kind plays out, the drama of avoiding anxiety and letting God grow the fruit of peace in us. The mundane can hardly even be called that anymore — now that word describes the events in which we struggle against terrible foes to reach the heights of heaven, battling ourselves, clawed at by the devil, and shoulder to shoulder with the Son of God himself.

That's why the Church is *catholic* — universal — because each and every life is drawn into that drama. In every moment, even the most boring, even the most dangerous, we stay near Jesus and listen to him, letting him live in us and guide us, and in giving ourselves to him we love; we become Love, because we are abiding in him and he is abiding in us; that brings us joy; and in that we find peace, that "freedom from outward disturbance" and "the calm of restless desire."

On the other hand, if we go about our everyday lives letting anxiety and worry cloud what we are doing, then our peace is disturbed; our joy flies away; our love turns inward and dies. If we are going to have and display joy, we must not allow ourselves to become anxious.

By the way, for those who still feel personally protective of Martha, it may help to remember that when Jesus is preparing to raise her brother Lazarus from the dead, it is Martha who sets the stage for the entire astounding event by being the one person out of the crowd who is so confident in the divine power and authority of Jesus that she knows he could easily raise Lazarus if he so chose. Mary, on the other hand, shows less confidence: "Lord, if you had been here, my brother would not have died" (John 11: 32). She has nothing else to say. So, the roles are reversed here: it is Martha who is free from anxiety, and Mary who is troubled.

Final score? Martha: 1; Mary: 1. A tie!

CHAPTER 5

ON NOT BEING ISSACHAR: OBSTACLE THREE

When Jacob is nearing death, he calls to his side his now-famous twelve sons (from whom the great tribes of Israel would derive their names) and says to them, "Gather around, that I may tell you what is to happen to you in the days to come" (Genesis 49:1, NAB).

Starting with Reuben, his oldest, Jacob tells each son something about themselves, some characteristic or destiny which can also be attributed to their descendants. Middle kid Judah gets the choicest message, including a comparison to lions and an assurance of royalty and abundance. That's fitting, since it is from the tribe of Judah that King David will come and, later, Jesus Christ.

Issachar, another of Jacob's sons, probably went away from his father's bedside a little less invigorated than Judah:

> Issachar is a rawboned ass,
>   crouching between the saddlebags.
> When he saw how good a settled life was,
>   and how pleasant the country,
> He bent his shoulder to the burden
>   and became a toiling serf.
> (Genesis 49:14 –15, NAB)

Yikes. "A rawboned ass." The ancient expression means someone who is strong — a good worker — but with no spirit, a beast of burden who is satisfied investing his life in relentless toil as long as he is stable and comfortable. Issachar has made an idol of a "settled life" in "a pleasant country." The result is that he has lost real freedom: all of his energy is in doing what the boss says, when the boss says, for the boss's purposes alone — *and the boss doesn't care about him.* The boss regards him only as a disposable tool for accomplishing work. The ironic consequence of all this is that Issachar never really gets to enjoy the benefits of a settled life in a pleasant country.

There is a lot of anxiety and boredom — and very little joy — that goes with that for any Issachar, whether he is slaving away for some overbearing landowner thousands of years ago or pushing numbers around on a computer screen in an anonymous gray-toned cubicle.

Pope Benedict XVI and all of his predecessors for over a hundred years have written about inhumane labor philosophies and the modern abuses of workers, and I do not claim to be qualified enough to add anything to that discussion. However, we can apply what has been written in a way that is germane to an exploration of the everyday attitudes and situations that block out the joy that Jesus is trying to grow in us.

How so? For one thing, because we can be such bad bosses to *ourselves*; we treat ourselves like Issachars. We get caught up in getting work done, forgetting the real meaning of work, and subjecting ourselves to relentless toil, which leaves us beaten down and anxiety-ridden and alienated from our own family and friends.

One way to guard against this is to put work in its proper context. I'm not only talking about our jobs that we get up and go to every day, but also about the dozens of ordinary domestic tasks for which we are responsible: cutting the grass, cleaning out the car, taking out the trash, and all the little things that can sweep us off our feet on any given day and carry us away in all kinds of crazy directions. It's all work. In order to regard it properly, as Christians, we would do well to ask: is doing work a holy thing?

In short, the Church says *yes*, but conditionally.

The Second Vatican Council's *Gaudium et Spes* ("Joy and Hope") looks at work relative to God, the Creator who gives each person the special ability to do what *he* does: to bring order out of chaos, to beautify, to build up, to improve. "When men and women provide for themselves and their families in such a way as to be of service to the community as well, they can rightly look upon their work as a prolongation of the work of the creator" (34).[10]

John Paul the Great, in *Laborem Exercens*, builds on that by looking at the issue, as he so often did, from the perspective of the human person. Work, on one hand, produces *objects* — a new car, a loaf of bread, a service like cable TV or unclogging a toilet, or some endeavor in the art world or the science world. This is the *objective* sense of work. On the other hand, we have the *subjective* sense of work: the objects are produced by a human being who is therefore the subject of the work. The *subjects* of work — you and me — because we are persons have an inherent dignity that flows from our spiritual natures, a dignity that can never be violated.[11]

See how this lays a huge burden of responsibility on the employer? He is forbidden to look at work only in the objective sense — seeing only the things that need to be done and the objects that need to be produced — to the exclusion of the subjective sense: that the people he employs are persons made in the image of God.

Expanding on that idea, we could add that this responsibility is also laid upon *me* as I direct *myself*. I am my own employer, so to speak. Every day I survey my world and see what needs to be done and then direct myself to do it, and sometimes I forget that I am in service to God and to my family. I start working in such a way that excludes God and my family: "I am going to finish cutting the grass right now and I don't care if my children all have high fevers and my wife got no sleep last night!!" Obviously, this disregards *them*. Suddenly they do not matter to me as much as the work itself. Work is meant to be a holy activity, but when it cuts off all the persons it is supposed to serve, especially God, and becomes merely an object that must be produced at all costs, it becomes unholy and an obstacle to joy.

In Pain

I can illustrate this with a glaring example from my own life.

I began my days as a rock musician with hardly anything in my heart except the subjective sense of the work involved in building a band and performing our songs. In other words, I wanted to make music *for* people: to thrill them or make them happy or make them laugh. Even the self-satisfaction I got was almost from a third-person perspective, as in: *isn't it great that musical guy is finding his place in the world?* I cherished the camaraderie in our band, *Pain*: the long, laughter-filled journeys from one state to the next, singing along to CDs and making vulgar jokes; the chaotic shows played in garishly-lit ramshackle clubs and loud bars with all eight of us squashed together blasting trumpets and slinging guitars and leaping around like gibbons. It was a tremendous experience of unity and joyful purpose. My cofounder and I were of one mind when it came to our goals for this strange (and strangely likable) musical act: we weren't in it to woo women, or to score drugs, or to get drunk, or to listen to ourselves play long, pointless guitar solos, or any of that junk that motivates some rockers. We wanted to make great music and see people enjoying it, happy in each other's company as we plied our trade.

A few years later, I was a different guy. I was addicted to pseudoephedrine, for one thing — I was taking a handful before every show so I could perform as wildly as I did in our early days. I had become secretly terrified of not being able to do that. I had come to stake my whole identity on being the frontman for this band. I had begun to treat my band mates as nothing other than raw material for me to use in order to get my songs made, performed, and produced. More and more I felt I owed nothing to anyone. I was twenty-nine years old, I weighed 128 pounds, and I was getting colds or infections about once every two months. The work involved in perpetuating the band, which was now only shorthand for my all-consuming ego and self-glorifying ambition, was all that mattered. Playing music, which had once been so selfless, had become something that was now almost completely *objective*, in the John Paul II sense: persons were excluded from consideration, even the long-buried authentic person that was me.

Anxiety, fear and desperation can lead each of us by the nose into doing all kinds of work in only this objective sense. Even in the most ordinary situations, we get the idea that *our work must be done no matter what — all life, time and space is depending on doing it now in this moment and if my rotten kids don't stop asking me to please make dinner, I'm going to explode and who could blame me??* Doing work *is* holy, but doing work as a substitute for holiness is unholy. It will kill joy in us and those around us.

Ora et Voluptatem

Obviously, an important way to keep from falling into the trap of improper work is to force yourself to enjoy periods of leisure (*voluptatem*). Many of us, frankly, are terrible leisure — we don't really know what to do with it and we often do not particularly want it. Regardless, the fact is that:

> Each one of us needs time and space for recollection, meditation and calmness.... Thanks be to God that this is so! In fact, this need tells us that we are not made for work alone, but also to think, to reflect or even simply to follow with our minds and our hearts a tale, a story in which to immerse ourselves, in a certain sense "to lose ourselves" to find ourselves subsequently enriched.[12]

On top of it all, we absolutely have to ground ourselves in prayer, the kind of prayerful spirit that doesn't allow itself to be permanently crowded out by daily chores. The Benedictines have an old, familiar motto: *ora et labora* — prayer and work. We are willing to do the *labora* part, but we leave aside the *ora* part. Without prayer and a spirit that is docile to the Holy Spirit, work becomes just fruitless suffering and even repetitive nonsense, accomplishing nothing more than what Thoreau said about it: just throwing stones over a wall only to walk to the other side and throw them back over, and over, and over. In prayer, even repetitive nonsense or all the gloomy tedious labor invented by the most heartless socialist regime can acquire sacredness.

Working for Joy

So … joy in work lies in respecting the person, the subject, of the work and in prayerfulness and genuine leisure. "Work is 'for man' and not man 'for work,'" wrote Blessed John Paul II,[13] and man is a spiritual creature made in the image of God who prays and thrives in the light of God above all things.

By the way, there is a completely legitimate, ancient, God-given way to indulge in loads of leisure and prayer: keep holy the Sabbath. Maybe you've seen those words inscribed on a stone tablet somewhere. It's not just a rule. It's a gift from a Father who doesn't want to see his children work themselves to physical or, especially, spiritual death.

CHAPTER 6

THE PLACE WHERE PAIN GOES: OBSTACLE FOUR

"Count it all joy ... when you meet various trials," writes St. James, "for you know that the testing of your faith produces steadfastness" (James 1:2–3).

Trials, we understand. Acknowledging that God uses them to make us steadfast — that's a little more difficult to accept, but, yes, alright. Counting it all *joy*, though? Suffering?

"Poverty, suffering and death is the way to him," says Brother Luc in Xavier Beauvois' *Of Gods and Men*. God help us all because it's just simply true, the way the face of a mountain is true for a grasshopper — meaning that there's no getting around it. This in no way means that we worship a god of poverty, suffering, and death, and we'll talk about that more as we go along. For now it is enough to say that poverty, suffering, and death is the lot of mankind, but when it is united to Christ it becomes a tool for our salvation, to the degree that we can say that we count it all joy.

From Out of the World

To help move a little further into this mystery, it might be a good idea to put aside, just for the moment, the dense theological formulations you've pored over and the long, complex arguments you've had with your atheist father-in-law over the problem of a God who allows suffering. Go back to them later. Right now, consider this very true story of what happened to my oldest sister, Susan, not long ago.

Today she is one of the Sisters of the Visitation, a Salesian order, living in a beautiful monastery in Mobile, Alabama, that is more than 175 years old. At the time of this writing she is a novice, so she wears a white veil instead of the black one she'll get after she takes her perpetual vows, and in it her face looks like a round pink and white apple. Her eyes twinkle. She is older than I by exactly ten years — we were born on the same date — yet she looks so youthful and joyful that a casual observer might seriously wonder who was born first.

Now go back just a few years. Imagine a woman in her mid-forties weeding a flowerbed in a courtyard. Her hair hangs in greasy strands. Her face is dark orange from the blood pounding in her head under the weight of a blazing, humid Alabama August. She cannot kneel, nor can she straighten her right leg, because of an accident at a sales conference in Quebec a few years prior, one of those absurd gatherings stocked with motivational speakers paid to boost everyone's morale. Susan was an enthusiastic attendee — that is her nature; she is energetic, upbeat, and eager to do good work. Unfortunately, during a part of the event in which an emcee directed everyone in footraces across a banquet room, Susan tripped and fell. The soft yet vital meniscus under both of her kneecaps ripped apart. As a result, and in spite of surgery and physical therapy, a dissonant chorus of painful sensations plays throughout her legs and back nearly without pause. She walks with a cane. She is unable to sleep in a bed — she sleeps in her recliner. She has no friends. Her husband died two years ago, and she works a bland job to support her only daughter, who is in high school.

It was during the time that her husband was in the hospital and succumbing to heart failure that Susan began to feel a vague pull to be a part of a religious order. She hardly even knew what that entailed, but she knew she had to explore the possibility. For most of her life she had been running from God because she always knew, deep down inside, that when it comes to him, it was all or nothing. That was too tall an order for she preferred to give him only pieces of herself, for occasional segments of time. As a result, her soul was fathoms full of dryness.

All of this led her, eventually, to one Father Cornelius, who became a good friend and a wise counselor as she tried to discover what God wanted her to do.

The parish where Father Cornelius served was very old and in bad repair, a situation that caught Susan's eye immediately. The grounds consisted of a chapel attached to a rectory and some empty offices with an enclosed courtyard between them. The courtyard used to be beautiful, presumably, perhaps in some pre-Vatican II era when nuns flitted around it like brown and white bumblebees. Now the place was a wreck. Crabgrass had the flowerbeds in a death grip. Weeds were rampant. Withered trash lay pasted against struggling shrubbery.

Susan decided that here was an opportunity to do something for God. She liked the idea of working outside of the chapel, close to the tabernacle, and beautifying things in the name of Jesus. Nothing much, but it was something. She would volunteer one hour a day — just one, no more. Her movements were severely limited, of course, but she was determined to adapt.

Digging in the Dirt

She had been at it for about two weeks, and the appearance of the place was definitely improving. Late summer flowers and ripe greenery reached up proudly from dark, clean turned earth and the stony ridges of flowerbeds were swept and cool from the water hose. Because of her knees, Susan had done it all from various bizarre bending poses or leaning on one elbow and reaching around the back of her head, like a game of Twister gone very wrong. Nevertheless, she had done a lot of good work. In fact, the sight of the courtyard inspired her to try, just try, to get down on her knees to continue. It hurt, of course, and she still could not straighten her leg, but she felt confident.

Feeling the rush of blood to starved veins felt good, and she took a deep, relieved breath. *This is good,* she thought, *this will work. If I'm just careful, this will work.*

When her hour was done, she tried to get back up.

What followed was an agony that Susan affirms was worse than childbirth. Fire throughout her legs. Something in her left knee split. Her back seized.

She knew something horrible had happened to her body, something irreversible. If she had ever thought there had been a chance that her knees might recover, that possibility now seemed gone forever.

At the same time, as she sat there sweating in the sun, she began to focus on some comforting notions. One was: *they are the Lord's knees, not mine. If they are meant to go, so be it.*

Why?

Because it's worth it, she realized. *It is worth it to be able to give this work to God.*

Susan's dirty, sweaty, orange face had blossomed into a grin, even as she held her cane in a grip that would choke a python and crawled toward her car like something from a movie about the undead. She had also become aware that Jesus was present, invisibly, along with his mother with whom Susan had never had a relationship before this day.

Driving home, with her body burning in pain, Susan could not stop smiling. *It's worth it.* When she got home, after the tedium of bathing and changing clothes, she lugged herself into her recliner and slept.

The Paradox of Pain

The next day, she went back to the chapel courtyard and gave another hour. She experienced the same blinding agony, even the fear that goes along with that kind of pain, the fear of your own weakness and mortality. *It's worth it.*

The day after that she went back again, still suffering the same amount of pain. Only this time she was no longer paying attention to it. She just, as always, tugged up weeds and raked away old paper wrappers with her gloved fingers.

That's ludicrous, we think. We can understand enduring pain, but only for a really good reason, some great cause like rescuing a boatload of children from burning wreckage or something. But enduring all of that agony for the sake of a few flowerbeds in a forgotten chapel courtyard? The proportions are all wrong, as we see it. How is this worth it?

To God, the size and dimensions of a work undertaken for his sake do not matter. Notice that I am not saying "the work doesn't matter, as long as we do it for God." The work *does* matter, and God wants us to do it as well as we can. What doesn't matter is if that work is, in the eyes of the world, small and insignificant. To him it is of eternal value. Giving that little work to God with all of her heart, all of her soul, and all of her mind, Susan experienced a joy that the most industrious tycoon holding sway over a multinational corporation likely never gets to have, for by her work and through it God was invited to be a full part of it — and he definitely accepted the invitation. She continued to be aware of his presence, and of Mary's, too, and she thought how wonderful it all was, and even after she dragged her sweating carcass home, she continued to believe that it was all worth it.

Sunrise

When she woke up the next day, she knew immediately that she'd had a good night's sleep. She eased carefully out of her recliner, but could not fail to notice that she was moving well. *Really* well. She didn't pay much attention to that fact, at first, since she was still preoccupied with the idea of giving all joyfully to God whether it hurt or not. After a little while there was just no way to ignore it anymore: the physical suffering she had endured for years and which had culminated in three days of excruciating agony was now just … gone. She could move without any trouble at all. Her back felt normal. She could bend and straighten her legs with perfect ease.

It occurred to her right away that she could, therefore, kneel, and that's exactly what she did, as part of a prayer of gratitude. She realized with a small start of surprise that she was thanking God for a miracle for which she had never asked.

She told our mom and dad eventually. Out of sheer habit she prefaced the tale with a junk pile of qualifications and disclaimers, but my dad gently waved all that away. "Don't analyze it. Accept it, and be grateful." He had learned lessons of his own about trusting in the gifts God gives us.

Each of us is subject to pain. God is with us there in those times because in Jesus he made himself subject to pain, too. The difference is that he makes his pain holy. At our choosing, he makes *our* pain holy, too.

The whole point of telling Susan's story is that when it comes to this idea called "redemptive suffering," explanations can never suffice. There simply is no substitute for the reality, for the lived experience. If you want to understand it, you have to give it a try.

Taste and See?

Pain is an obstacle to joy — unless that pain is suffered in Christ Jesus. Then, behold, it becomes a *cause* for joy. It is that simple, but putting it into practice is the most difficult thing you could do.

There is a verse from Psalm 34 that tells us to "taste and see that the LORD is good" (v. 8). You've no doubt heard it thrown around or sung in a hymn somewhere or other, but it never seems to get the proper treatment, it seems to me. The intention behind the way it is often used is to make us aware that God's ways are sweetly pleasant, and we ought to acknowledge and give thanks for that.

Only that isn't really right. The psalm in question is attributed to King David after he escapes the clutches of Achish, King of Gath. The story is told in the first book of Samuel. He escapes the king not by some feat of acrobatics or by lopping off his enemies' heads, but by the practical expediency of pretending to be completely insane. He flops around Achish's throne room, drooling all over himself and babbling, and Achish says to his servants, "Do I not have enough madmen, that you bring in this one to carry on in my presence?" (1 Samuel 21:15, NAB). David is allowed to leave, and readers can decide for themselves whether or not this tactic might be worth trying the next time you are summoned to civil court for unpaid traffic tickets.

Regardless, the author of 1 Samuel then goes on to tell us that David gathered with his family in a cave, and there he "was joined by all those who were in difficulties or in debt, or who were embittered, and he became their leader" (22:2, NAB).

This, then, is the context for the psalm that tells us to taste and see the goodness of the Lord: a man and his followers who were in defeat, in difficulties and in debt and embittered, singing "In my misfortune I called, the LORD heard and saved me" (Psalm 34:7, NAB). The "taste" or "savor" of God is not something immediately pleasant. It is not as if the psalmist was saying the equivalent of: "Look, here's a freshly made chocolate pudding pie! Taste and see the goodness!" The psalmist, in essence, is saying: "I am hurting, I am out of money, I am heartsick — yet I am going to honestly and without reserve call out to God and let him guide my life."

Making such a pledge will not likely produce instantaneous joy, since God is not a Happy Pill. The New American Bible's translation of the verse is instructive: "Learn to savor how good the LORD is" (Psalm 34:9). *Learn* to savor — a process of suffering that will lead to deeper closeness with the Lord. There is even a process of suffering involved in the mere act of submitting to God — after all, you are in pain, which makes you panicky and untrusting. Just to let go of *that* hurts. Then, even when you do it, your problems are still with you. You are still in difficulty, in debt, and embittered. But the goodness of the Lord will begin to become apparent to you; without totally realizing it you will be drawn closer to him.

Once you've taken that step, you will find — though probably not right away — that counting as joy the suffering that brought you there is not nearly as ludicrous a suggestion as it might once have seemed.

The Strange and the Wonderful

The people who have taken the Christian challenge to follow Jesus into the heart of suffering belong to a thundercloud of witnesses. Some of them we may know personally, the way I know my sister, Susan. Others have passed on and acquired world-class status — we call them saints. "How gloriously different all the saints," wrote C.S. Lewis, contrasting them with the monotonous similitude of all the tyrants of history. It is undeniably true. So many holy men and women, so many that most of us have forgotten most of them, so many that they crowd out the empty spaces on our parish liturgical calendars, and yet each of them bursting with life and color, and all expressing the joy of God.

St. Paul. He could be prickly. We know that from his own writings. But we also know, thanks to his Second Letter to the Corinthians, that he received the dreaded "thirty-nine lashes" not once, not twice, but five separate times. Three times he was beaten with rods. He survived a stoning, three shipwrecks, "danger from rivers, danger from robbers, danger from my own people, danger from Gentiles, danger in the city … in the wilderness … at sea … danger from false brethren; in toil and hardship, through many a sleepless night, in hunger and thirst, often without food, in cold and exposure" (11:26–27). And what does this miserable wretch claim to be filled with? Bitterness? Resentment? Outrage at God? No to all three. He claims to be "filled with comfort.… I am overjoyed" (7:4).

St. Lawrence. If you have never been cooked alive, make sure you ask St. Lawrence about it when you reach heaven. The well-worn story goes that when this third-century deacon of Rome was being roasted on a spit, he turned to his personal chefs and said something like, "You may want to turn me — I think I'm done on this side."

St. John Vianney. He "frequently went into the fields and kissed the ground for joy,"[14] and yet, for some reason, what sticks with me about St. John Vianney is his joyful disregard for the natural problems that affected him as he reached old age. For instance, all his teeth fell out. For most people, losing teeth is both a source of extreme embarrassment and an incontrovertible sign that future meals will include less steak and more tapioca. St. John Vianney kept right on giving sermons to huge throngs. His entire body slowly fell apart as his parishioners watched, but it didn't seem to perturb him much. Father George Rutler points out that the good Curé of Ars "thought it fun when his legs collapsed, chuckling that he was like a drunkard."[15]

St. Francis of Assisi. Chesterton writes about when the incomparable St. Francis made his fateful decision to kick away everything the world had to offer and put his faith utterly in God:

> He went out half-naked in his hair-shirt into the winter woods, walking the frozen ground.... He was penniless, he was parentless, he was to all appearance without a trade or a plan or a hope in the world; and as he went under the frosty trees, he burst suddenly into song.[16]

St. Faustina. This strange, sweet lady, who is referred to as the Apostle of the Divine Mercy, might seem like an unsuitable choice for this list. She seems to spend the bulk of her gargantuan *Diary* suffering or enraptured by some mystical vision, and you get the impression that an ordinary conversation with her might have left you feeling like you had just watched a Stanley Kubrick marathon. In spite of that, I sense profound joy in St. Faustina. I think she is a great representative of those who are *quietly* joyful. In fact, her opinion was that "a talkative soul is empty inside,"[17] and Jesus himself assured her: "Bring your ear close to my Heart, forget everything else, and meditate upon my wondrous mercy."[18] Yet it's impossible to think of her as simply reclusive or antisocial. She cared about everyone, including the souls in Purgatory, but Jesus was the blazing center of her world. Thanks to her docility and perseverance souls continue to discover how wide God's mercy really is.

St. Maximilian Kolbe. In Auschwitz for giving shelter to Jews, Father Maximilian Kolbe calmly requested that he be allowed to suffer punishment on behalf of a fellow prisoner. The Nazis accommodated his request. He was transferred to solitary confinement and deliberately starved. Shrunken skin on cold bones, dark circles under eyes, round glasses and a shaved head — this was Father Kolbe in his dark cell, side by side with a few other wretched souls. Death was imminent; it would come in the form of a syringe full of carbolic acid, but until then guards strolling past the cell distinctly heard its occupants *singing songs* of joy and hope, led by Father Kolbe.[19] That is what is meant when we say that the fruit of the Holy Spirit is delicious and ripe even when the world around us has turned into Mordor.

The foregoing are saints. By definition these are people who do what everybody else says can't be done. Their stories can be uplifting, but they can also be irritating. Saints scandalize us. They are supposed to. Their lives are not meant primarily as an instruction manual for us on how to live, but to show us that a saintly life is both what we are supposed to be striving for *and* attainable.

CHAPTER 7

CALLING FOR REINFORCEMENTS

*Men need to
learn to
stay strong
Be spiritual love
CATHOLIC
EVANGELISTS
.cov*

*Primary
vocation
is to
Love*

*Primary goal
of church is
to evangelize*

———

I am a failed carpenter, and my wife knows it. She has watched me build any number of wooden structures, usually furniture, using all the right tools and filled with unflappable enthusiasm, only to end up with humiliating wobbly, misshapen things from a Dr. Suess book. You wouldn't risk setting an empty coffee cup on them.

The reason is always the same: I don't double-check and reinforce what I'm building as I go along.

I would like to avoid this error in my writing — or at least in this book. It occurs to me that some of the points I've covered so far might benefit from a little reinforcement. To handle this, I've brought in a few imaginary objectors, voicing real and very common objections.

Being Joyful in Battle

Question: "You wrote in an earlier chapter that anxiety has no business in the life of a Christian, and that we should be consistently joyful. But what about those times when a person is in a really chaotic situation, like a war or a medical emergency or just a day when everything is moving at a ludicrous speed and you can't catch a break? It's quite a stretch to say I can be joyful in times like that. I'm not talking about the Maximilian Kolbe situations where death is slowly, inexorably settling around you. I mean: the frantic times, with bullets (either metaphorical or literal) firing past you and everybody yelling and no time to kneel down somewhere and pray."

A nswer: I would rephrase the question: can one have the peace and satisfaction that comes from possessing God (which is what true joy is) even in the face of tumult and death? The answer is: yes.

Of *course* we are going to fail repeatedly and give in to anxiety, though. Only God is perfect, and we are not synonymous with God. God lives in us, however, and he is patiently growing the fruits of holiness in us. Our job is to get back up on our feet every single time after we fall and ask him to please keep working on us. In other words, what is required of us is simple perseverance. Also, we build up our strength when we consciously practice not being anxious, especially when anxiety comes in lower, less challenging waves. In time, by God's grace, a faithful person will know joy even in the face of doom.

At the risk of overdoing it on inspirational models, I submit for your consideration one who is, to my mind, one of the reigning champions of being joyful in battle: Judas Maccabeus.

This is one of those times when I feel kind of sorry for my Protestant brothers and sisters out there, because they don't include Maccabees 1 and 2 in their Bibles. That's too bad — they are well worth reading. The books tell the story of how the Israelites, in the second century B.C., found themselves under the thumb of yet another despot, Antiochus IV of the Greek Seleucid dynasty. Antiochus invaded the great city of Jerusalem and slaughtered, plundered, burned and terrorized at will. The Israelites' religious freedom, so intensely precious to them, was ripped away by this king of thugs, and their temple was ruthlessly desecrated, including the eventual placement of an altar to Zeus in the Holy of Holies. "And there was great mourning for Israel, in every place where they dwelt, and the rulers and the elders groaned" (1 Maccabees 1:25, NAB).[20]

A Jewish priest, Mattathias, looked around at the bloody corpses of his friends and relatives, at the scorched walls of Jerusalem, and above all at the awful sacrilege that had been committed against the Holy Temple and decided to fight back, "for our lives and our traditions" (2:40). Eventually, one of his sons, Judas Maccabeus, took charge of things and continued the fierce and brilliant revolt his father had begun. "All his brothers and all who had joined his father supported him," Scripture tells us, "and they carried on Israel's war joyfully" (3:2).

The enemy wasn't going to take all this lying down, of course. A commander named Seron gathered a massive army for a counterattack: "Judas went out to meet them with a few men." Those few men, understandably, were aghast at the swarming hordes of Seron's warriors.

"How can we, few as we are, fight such a mighty host as this?" (3:16–17).

Judas's response is comparable to *Henry V*'s famous St. Crispin Day speech in its intensity and its call to heroic courage, yet it is also suffused with a sublime reliance on and confidence in almighty God:

> "It is easy for many to be overcome by a few; in the sight of Heaven there is no difference between deliverance by many or by few; for victory in war does not depend upon the size of the army, but on strength that comes from Heaven. With great presumption and lawlessness they come against us to destroy us and our wives and children and to despoil us; but we are fighting for our lives and our laws. [The Lord] himself will crush them before us; so do not be afraid of them." When he finished speaking, he rushed suddenly upon Seron and his army, who were crushed before him. (3:18–23, NAB)

Anxiety comes upon us all in overwhelming situations because our shortsighted eyes see an unstoppable force — anxiety seems reasonable. Yet the truth is that we should all feel offended, as Judas Maccabeus was, that the devil is "trying to destroy us" and everything we hold dear. Most important, we should recognize that the devil is as easily defeated by God as a gnat is incinerated by a flamethrower; if we remain in Christ, the devil has no power over us at all. God's will may, in fact, include all ʌds of calamity in our lives, but if we belong to him, ʌ there is nothing whatsoever to be anxious about.

We should qualify that. Judas Maccabeus and his brothers were not successful simply because they professed a love for God and had a lot of great intentions. They prayed constantly, they fasted (yes, literally), they made atonement for sins and stayed "zealous for the law" (2:27). If we desire the peace that is the opposite of anxiety, these practices are vital to the process of Jesus saving us and growing fruit in us. If we neglect our part, we can't expect peace or joy.

Does Prayer Work?

Question:You have written a lot in this book about praying to God and suffering prayerfully, and you almost make it sound like God responds to prayer as clearly and promptly as the local pizza delivery place when I call to put in an order. I have no experience of that. It isn't just that prayer feels tedious and unnatural but, worse than that, it doesn't work. When my wife had cancer last year, I prayed every day for five months. I did two novenas — one through the intercession of St. Joseph, the other through the intercession of Mary.

You know what happened? My wife died. I saw her in her last moments — her mouth stretched back into a silent howl and her eyes shut like Venus flytraps and she shuffled right off this mortal coil. I can tell you right now: prayer doesn't work. And, by the way, that statement doesn't make me an atheist. I'm just realistic about what God is. He's all-powerful, and he's changeless. Prayer isn't going to change his mind. He's going to do exactly what he wants to do exactly when he wants to do it, and an ocean of prayers isn't going to move him one way or the other. So, why pray for anything? God doesn't change — even Plato knew that. I say: let him carry out his plan — I have no idea what it is, I don't want to know. I just want to get along, pay my bills, take care of my family, and live my life. God will do what he wants."

Answer: Generally, people who talk or think like this do not start off their lives that way. They get there because they have been disappointed. They expected something from God; he didn't deliver; now they are angry and resentful. They do not know what to do with God anymore, so they push him away and tell themselves that they are being realistic and pragmatic. But chances are, before all that, they tried seriously to abandon themselves to God's will, to trust him like little children. They won't admit that now, though, because they are bitter.

More to the point, why do we pray to God for things at all? A priest friend of mine once told me that he prays because that's what his heart wants to do. He desires to pray to God, and to tell him everything, and ask for everything. What's more, the New Testament from one end to the other encourages us to pray all the time, for all we want or need, and for its various authors the fact that God is changeless seems to have no bearing on the issue at all.

That is because although God *is* changeless, the *world* isn't. God made it that way. It is in constant flux — not just in terms of time passing and mountains slowly crumbling, but even the surface on which you are standing or sitting right now is just a plane of mostly space with a comparatively few vibrating atoms held together by electromagnetic attraction. It was God who made this world. The almighty, unchangeable "I Am" Who Can't Not Exist made a whole universe that changes all the time.

So, how is the changeless God actively involved with us? It's mysterious, I grant you, but St. Thomas Aquinas describes it this way: we are houses, living, moving houses, and God is the sun. We have been given the power to turn and let the sun in our windows — or to shut it out. But the sun is always the same.[21]

This means that, in the way that God has the power to cause things, we humans, created in his image and likeness, also have the power to cause things. We can cause changes in ourselves and, to a degree, in others, in those people whom God brings in and out of our lives. With those goals in mind I ask for God to make changes to the world, and particularly to that part of the world that is *me*.

Of course he's going to say "no" to me sometimes — do I know best what's needed, or does he? At the end of the day what's important is not how many times he granted me exactly what I pleaded for in prayer, but how close I came to being like Jesus, how closely I aligned my windows with the Eternal Sun. To be obedient is to be like Jesus, as is being humble and docile to the Holy Spirit. If I'm carrying around the opposite of those things in my heart — disobedience, pride, and willfulness, all carefully disguised as resignation ("I'll just get along and live my life and let God do what he wants"), then the problem isn't merely that I will live a joyless life, but that I have chosen to walk apart from our Father. Walking along with Jesus whe ever he leads, even if it's down the *via dolorosa*, is how we discover joy, not by having our personal desires granted.

Joy Is for Sissies

Question: My heroes are Padre Pio, Jerome, Benedict, Paul: tough-skinned, serious guys not renowned for their joyful ebullience. I don't like prayer groups, Bible study groups, bake sales, or other community gatherings where people tend to be very chirpy about their relationship with Jesus. If that's joy, I'm fine without it.

Answer: Once again, joy doesn't mean giddiness or chirpiness. It is the peace and satisfaction that comes from possessing God. This may or may not express itself as a big, shiny grin, or as laughter, or as excitement, or as a shout. For some it does. For others it means getting very quiet — they become captivated by the deep ocean of love that is God whom they perceive in their souls. If that's you, then congratulations. But distinguish between that and the mere anti-social curmudgeonliness that was, no doubt, among the crosses saints like Jerome and Benedict had to bear.

> Once again, joy doesn't mean giddiness or chirpiness. It is the peace and satisfaction that comes from possessing God. This may or may not express itself as a big, shiny grin, or as laughter, or as excitement, or as a shout.

We are all called to community in Christ. Just because we are naturally reclusive doesn't excuse us — and, believe me, I can sympathize. So can a friend of mine who is a parish priest, who once told me in private: "*The people*, Dan ... I could be a holy man if not for all the people." He was half-kidding, because he knew how preposterous his statement was. But he was half-serious, too — and that, I think, is why he made every effort to continually place himself at everyone's disposal, to meet everybody who came to him with joy and undivided attention. You may not be able to reach that level of community involvement, and for those of us who aren't parish priests we likely will never be called to. But we have to be ready to submit everything about us to God's will, including the discomfort we feel around all those jabbering, annoying, time-consuming people who sweep in and out of our personal space.

What's With All the Suffering?

Question: You've talked extensively about Jesus' suffering, and how we must enter into that mystery in order to find joy and, frankly, I still am very uncomfortable with it.

Answer: I would be shocked if you weren't! It is an uncomfortable reality. As we try to acclimate ourselves to it, one pitfall is that we sometimes confuse true joy with the mere act of "putting on a happy face," being optimistic, being cheerful and upbeat. Those are good qualities and true gifts — but they are not the same things as Christian joy. The danger is that you can go along thinking that your natural gifts of cheerfulness are synonymous with the joy of the Holy Spirit. Then when your cheerfulness inevitably runs out, you think God has abandoned you. Submit everything to God, even your natural virtues. Everything.

"Okay, but that doesn't address the emphasis on Jesus' suffering. I don't like to talk about suffering. Suffering hurts. Jesus doesn't like pain and suffering — he went through it, yes, for us, for our salvation, but isn't it kind of morbid and obsessive to always be talking about it? It's like Lent 24/7 for some Catholics! How is that joyful?"

You're right — there *is* the danger of becoming fixated on suffering, and that's not good. There are various reasons a person might fall into this trap: a lack of trust in God, perhaps, or having a disproportionate expectation of themselves, thinking that it is they who must suffer more in order to reach heaven.

Early twentieth-century Catholic convert Edith Stein noted the inherent creepiness of being fixated on suffering: "For by nature, a person flees from suffering. And the mania for suffering caused by a perverse lust for pain differs completely from the desire to suffer in expiation. Such lust is not a spiritual striving, but a sensory longing no better than other sensory desires, in fact worse because it is contrary to nature."[22]

But notice that she is very clear that the desire *to suffer in expiation* is a good thing. Why? How is that different? Because it's not for you — it's for others. Jesus suffers for others — he puts his entire earthly life into that one, focused mission. As followers of Jesus, we have to tackle suffering the way he did: purposefully, lovingly, for the sake of others. We "complete what is lacking in Christ's afflictions" (Colossians 1:24), which means that I personally must endure my sufferings in a way that is loving and obedient to God. By this I become slowly purified and I help others to become purified as well — all through the grace of God. That's the amazing way in which he allows us to participate in Jesus' saving mission.

We definitely must not seek out suffering as if it were a kind of hard liquor that stings going down but gives us a nice, warm feeling of euphoria — that's exactly the kind of thing Edith Stein was criticizing. In *A Man for All Seasons*, when young Margaret assumes that her saintly father, Thomas More, will publicly denounce the king's insidious new oath being forced upon everyone, Thomas doesn't puff up his chest and proclaim loudly, "Yes, I'll eagerly embrace the terrible suffering that will come with that decision, because I'm a Catholic!" In fact, he insists on first examining the exact wording of the oath to see if it will be possible to just say the damned thing. More's family is confused — this seems like cowardice. "Our natural business," Thomas gravely replies, "lies in escaping."[23] He clearly parks his car in the same garage as Edith Stein: it is our God-given nature to flee from suffering, not seek it out.

But when suffering *does* come, when there's no more getting around it and it has you on the cross, then *choose* it. Love it, in the way that "love" means seeking the good of the other. Ask Jesus to take it and make it his own and, in that way that only he can do, turn it into something that helps us and others. That's *redemptive* suffering. It is the greatest, most loving thing we can do during our short lives on earth, therefore it is worth thinking about, reading about, meditating on, planning for, and strategizing over — not for suffering's sake, but for the fruit it produces. It's the *fruit* we're after.

Unfortunately, when we put our hearts and minds to this task, people will misunderstand us — we run the risk of being lumped in with people who really do fixate on suffering. But we aren't fixating on suffering, are we? We're fixating on Love. The evidence of that will be the joy in us, "a strong and pure joy,"[24] as Edith Stein observed.

CHAPTER 8

ABANDONMENT TO GOD'S WILL

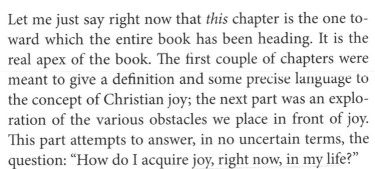

Let me just say right now that *this* chapter is the one toward which the entire book has been heading. It is the real apex of the book. The first couple of chapters were meant to give a definition and some precise language to the concept of Christian joy; the next part was an exploration of the various obstacles we place in front of joy. This part attempts to answer, in no uncertain terms, the question: "How do I acquire joy, right now, in my life?"

I've been heavily hinting at it for several chapters. The way to acquire joy, the only way — and there is no other way — is to completely abandon yourself to God's will.

That's it. There is no other answer.

"Father ... not my will, but yours, be done" (Luke 22:42, NAB), said Jesus in Gethsemane, as the darkest hour in all human history was closing in on him. The Holy Spirit inspired the Gospel writers to record those words so that we would all understand how vital it is to see that we must abandon our will.

As I said in my introduction, I do not pretend to be an "athlete," that is, an expert in Christian joy. Neither am I a hero of abandoning my will. Therefore, I think it is especially important to pass along the wisdom of a truly great Christian who *did* abandon himself to God's will and who shines with the joy that is the result. He was crushed by evil — crushed — and yet he submitted to God. Such people don't seem possible; we don't usually see them in our day-to-day lives, so their lives become like a fairy tale. But they are real. Their reality challenges us to either imitate them or sink down into the mediocre swamp with which so many have become contented.

Led into the Dark

Walter Ciszek was a Jesuit priest from Pennsylvania, born of Polish immigrants in 1904. He had spent time as a gang member, so it was a shock when he decided to enter the priesthood. Eventually, he was sent to the city of Albertyn, in Poland, only to see it fall into the cold-blooded hands of Stalinist Russia. Father Ciszek, having long been attracted to the idea of ministering to the oppressed people of Russia, now saw his chance. After securing the proper approval, he travelled over the border and settled in the town of Chusovoy under a fake name to work as a logger — all so he could secretly minister to the people there.

In 1941 he was ratted out and taken prisoner. He was sent to the dread Lubianka Prison, where "men were broken … in body and spirit."[25] Father Ciszek spent *five* years there. He was regularly tortured and kept in isolation. After that he spent *fifteen* years doing bone-wrenching labor in a freezing gulag of Siberia. He did his best to minister to souls, but he was also surrounded by some of the most foul, wicked men imaginable, men who had become animals in order to endure captivity. Father Ciszek experienced the lowest depths of anguish, despair, and misery. Yet he persevered in faith, and through grace he slowly matured in his relationship with God.

Going into his ordeal, he thought he knew a good bit about what it was to abandon his will to God. In his memoir, *He Leadeth Me*, he writes:

> At times of crisis, especially, I had tried to discover his will and to follow it to the best of my ability.... Up until now, I had always seen my role ... as an active one.... I had retained in my own hands the reins of all decisions, actions, and endeavors.... God's will was "out there" somewhere, hidden, yet clear and unmistakable. It was my role — man's role — to discover what it was and then conform my will to that ... I remained ... in essence the master of my own destiny. Perfection consisted simply in learning to discover God's will in every situation and then bending every effort to do what must be done.
>
> Now, with sudden and almost blinding clarity and simplicity, I realized I had been trying to do something with my own will and intellect that was at once too much and mostly all wrong. God's will was not hidden somewhere "out there" in the situations in which I found myself; *the situations themselves* were *his will for me.* He was asking of me

an act of total trust, allowing for no interference or restless striving on my part, no reservations, no exceptions, no areas where I could set conditions or seem to hesitate. He was asking a complete gift of self, nothing held back ... it is not really a question of trust in God at all, for we want very much to trust him; it is really a question of our ultimate belief in his existence and his providence, and it demands the purest act of faith."[26]

The Will to Allow

So, God's will is in the situations that we encounter in our lives. None of us has a problem acknowledging this when we turn a corner and come face-to-face with a sweet old lady who needs seventy-five cents for the bus — we give her the money, we help her on to the bus, we give her little wrinkled hand a squeeze, and then off we go, praising God for the way he brings those kinds of situations to our attention. *That*, we say confidently, was God's will — that we should meet *that* particular person at *exactly* the right time and blah blah blah.

But what about when we're on our way to work and we get a flat tire?

That's not God's will! That's just stupid, meaningless suffering ... that's the fault of the tire maker ... and why now, anyway? It's the worst time, since I have a big appointment this morning. No God of love would do this to me!

What Father Ciszek realized, though, there in the hellish prisons of Communist Russia, is that every situation that comes along in your life falls within God's will. The flat tire falls within God's will, even if its collapse was directly the result of shoddy work by lazy, ignorant people at a tire making plant. The point here is not to make a sudden deep-water exploration of the mystery of evil in the world, but simply to acknowledge that God knew your tire would go flat right then — and he allowed it. It was his will to allow it. The question now becomes: how will you respond?

We can all imagine worse problems than flat tires, of course. People suffer things that are too horrible to let loose within the imagination. Once again: this is not the proper place to attempt a full investigation of the mystery of evil. For now the goal is only to wrap our minds around what Father Ciszek discovered: that God's will for us lies in the things we experience.

Even so, the mind recoils in horror. Part of the reason is because it sees a rigid, judgmental God sitting coldly aloof while his children are being eaten. He is *not* aloof, though — when Jesus appeared to Saul, who was hunting down Christians, and said "Saul, Saul, why do you persecute me?" (Acts 9:4), he wasn't being poetic. Nor is the name "Emmanuel" a mere token — God *is* with us, suffering with us, taking the sin and wickedness and pain of everyone upon himself right along with us. He is one with us.

Finding the Secret God

That begs the question: "Why do I have to go through this at all?"

That's a big question, and I can't answer it thoroughly. Anybody who says they can is selling something. But there are answers that help: he is purifying us, he is making us stronger, he is healing people through our suffering, he is bringing about a greater good than we can imagine. Though we are left unsatisfied by these answers, we know he is suffering with us, which he does because he loves us, and that should earn a little trust from us.

Although, as Father Csizek points out, it isn't ultimately a matter of trust, is it? When loved ones are dying, when debt is piling up, when disease is running wild, what nags at us is the question: "Are you there *at all*? Is there really any kind of an actual plan you have going?" If we knew that, if we could just be sure that he's there, and that this is all going somewhere intelligible — then, of course, trust would come more easily and we would more readily abandon our will to his.

But right there is the big, scandalous secret that stymies so many people. God is hidden. If we want to find him, the real God, the God who is Love, then we have to become accustomed to his way of doing things. He wants you to know him, and love him, and serve him, and so he reveals himself through people, places and things — all the stuff of the world he created. But above all, the hidden God secretly knocks on the door of our heart.

"Behold," says Christ in Revelation, "I stand at the door and knock; if any one hears my voice and opens the door, I will come in to him and eat with him, and he with me" (3:20). St. Francis de Sales, in his *Introduction to the Devout Life*, refers to this knocking at the door as "inspiration." It is a three-part process, as he explains it: Jesus knocks on the door, you open it with joy, and then you immediately begin doing whatever it was he was knocking on your door about in the first place.

St. Francis differentiates between hearing the Word of God through good counsel or homilies or stories about saints; this is more direct. Jesus himself has come to you to urge you to do something or to avoid something, or to bless you or to enlighten you about something — "everything that sends us on our way to our everlasting welfare."

Yes, that's right: I am asserting and emphasizing that it is a normative part of a faithful Christian life to be guided by God on a daily basis. As the situations and experiences of life that are God's will roll upon us one after another, he comes to us in the silence of our hearts to lead us through them.

What's Real?

How do we know when it is really God speaking to us and when it is one or both of the two enemies in our lives as identified by Dr. Kreeft (namely, the devil and/or us)?

To ask that question is no small thing, not only because it is important for figuring out how to move ahead in choosing to be the joyful people we were created to be, but also because it means we've made the long journey from "Is God really there?" to "Okay, so what does he want?" We're therefore ready to hear the Church's wisdom on weeding out false inspirations from true ones and then abandoning our will to God as he leads us. That means putting those inspirations into action, particularly in the practice of virtue. All that waits in the chapter ahead.

CHAPTER 9

IN ACTION

—

Abandonment of will is not an exercise in turning off our brains and inflating ourselves with lots of nice, airy feelings about the Lord. It requires us to act, using every gift that God has given us to the utmost of our ability. By our actions (performed with abandonment to God's will) we begin to more fully possess and exhibit joy, the fruit of the Holy Spirit.

To help us in the brass tacks of abandonment there is almost no end of saints and mentors and spiritual guides out there. They are God's gift to you — so keep your eye out for the ones with whom he wants you to connect. In general, you will need to apply yourself to two big categories: recognizing genuine inspirations and practicing virtue.

Recognizing Genuine Inspirations

In the last chapter we referred to St. Francis de Sales' guidance on how the inspiration process works:

1. Jesus knocks on the door of your heart; a beautiful image that conveys the idea of God proposing something to you that he'd like you to work toward.

2. You open the door with joy — that's "with joy;" it takes practice, but to not receive inspirations with joy is to stare at Jesus on your doorstep mumbling about whether it's really him or not and if this really is the best time and wouldn't he like to come back later when it's more convenient because then you'll have the house cleaned up and so on. It's just rude to do anything other than be joyful when the King of the Universe stops by.

3. You receive him. You begin working on whatever it is he would like you to do.

These representations are certainly rich and vivid but, admittedly, the fact is that the whole thing is very subtle. The voice of God does not come in the storm, or the earthquake, or the fire — he is the still, small voice quietly proposing things to you. Not forcing, but proposing, inviting. How to recognize that voice in a loud, obnoxious world?

First, we have to keep ourselves pure. We cannot have one foot in a life of Christian discipleship and the other foot in a life of sexual perversion, materialism, gluttony, or power mongering — that just doesn't work. No one can serve two masters. Either get with the program or don't, but don't think you can surreptitiously lead a sinful half-life and still be able to hear Jesus knocking on the door. You won't hear a thing — you'll be too busy way back in a spiritual recess, some interior cave, doling out pieces of your immortal soul to various members of a passing parade of distractions. Stay pure.

Even in doing that, the devil isn't going to just hang back and let you have breezy daily interactions with Jesus on the front door of your heart. He will regularly send Jesus-shaped devils to your doorstep with their own suggestions. How to spot them? St. Francis de Sales has some pointers.

His *Treatise on the Love of God* is particularly useful if you are weighing some decision and two or more options appear equally worthy. The following is a small example of how to go about bringing your decision into conformity with God's will:

1. "Avoid undertaking too many spiritual works at once."[27] If you find yourself jumping from one project to the next without finishing previous projects it is a strong sign that you are being led on a wild goose chase by impulses not placed in you by God. Have one or two paths in mind and follow them with perseverance.

2. "Follow only those inspirations that are holy and that bring your soul peace." Of the two or more options you are considering, which one brings you peace of mind, makes you feel at ease? One caveat here is that a peaceful inspiration can also come with a sense of urgency. Sometimes the Holy Spirit says: "I'd like you to do something for me, and it needs to be done right now, not

five minutes from now." That's basically what he said to Philip in the Acts of the Apostles — whatever Philip was doing at that moment, he had to drop it immediately and run to catch up with the Ethiopian's chariot (8:27–30). Philip had to move quickly — but the urge was still only a peaceful proposal from God, not an anxiety-ridden shove by the devil. Learning the difference only comes through practice.

3. "When following inspirations, always obey the authority of the Church." Obedience is not a virtue we're fond of, but it is an absolute necessity in the spiritual life. For the purposes of making a big decision in life, let me recommend calling up your favorite priest or other spiritual advisor and simply telling him your plan. He may advise against it; if he's your usual go-to person for sage advice, then chances are he's right. But here's the key: *note your own reaction if he advises against your planned path.* Is your reaction one of anger, resentment, and intransigence? St. Francis de Sales warns us that those reactions are clear indicators that your impulse is *not* from God: "A man who says that he is inspired and then refuses to obey his superiors is an impostor."

This is tough — it seems like we might be exalting men above the Holy Spirit. But remember that the Church is only what she is because she has been given the authority of the Holy Spirit. "I will give you the keys to the kingdom of heaven" (Matthew 16:19), Jesus said to Peter. It would be awfully confusing if the Holy Spirit said, "Listen to the Church — that's me talking!" But then turned around said, "Ignore the Church — listen to what I'm saying *now*." So he doesn't do that.

There's so much more, of course. The bottom line is: if we want peace and true joy, we'll have to work at recognizing God's will because it's only there that we'll find them. The uncomfortable fact is that his will might often be contrary to our own, but if we don't conform to it we will not be happy.

> The bottom line is: if we want peace and true joy, we'll have to work at recognizing God's will because it's only there that we'll find them. The uncomfortable fact is that his will might often be contrary to our own....

Practicing Virtue

Joy in action involves practicing virtue; the Church gives us all kinds of guides for doing so. Among the more famous ones are the venerable Corporal Works of Mercy and Spiritual Works of Mercy. As the name suggests, the Corporal Works have to do with the body: feed the hungry, give drink to the thirsty, clothe the naked, shelter the homeless, visit the sick, visit the imprisoned, and bury the dead. The Spiritual Works are: correct the sinner, teach the ignorant, counsel the doubtful, comfort the sorrowful, bear wrongs patiently, forgive those who hurt you, and pray for the living and the dead. The beneficiaries of any or all of these works are "the poor," which we may define as "anyone who lacks what the Corporal and Spiritual Works aim to supply."

Imagine if we didn't just read those lists but actually did them. What if we took the time to consider how we might apply each one in a simple way every day? Jesus does not just suggest them to us, after all — he demands them. He ties eternal salvation to them, and those who ignore them are in serious jeopardy of not going to heaven (see, for instance, Matthew 25:31–46). Jesus must be serious about them.

In fact, Christians *do* take them seriously — I see it all the time. I am frequently the recipient of charitable works by Christians who, whether they know it or not, are fulfilling the Corporal and Spiritual Works of Mercy in a hundred little ways. On a grander scale there is the case of Katie Davis who moved from the United States to Africa, became the legal guardian for thirteen abandoned, homeless Ugandan children, and is living there with them as their loving, nurturing mother, and all because she took Jesus' commandments seriously.[28]

How many people fail to respond when Jesus calls them to do something as bold and definitively life-changing as that? I am not qualified to know — I don't *want* to know. I know that I personally am not called to travel to Africa like Katie Davis or to Calcutta like Blessed Mother Teresa — my call is to more immediate regions. I suspect that is true for most of us.

That does not mean, of course, that we can ignore the people who live in distant poor areas. We pray for them, put money in the baskets at church, and put a little aside for worthy charities (making double sure that they *are* worthy). The lion's share of our attention, however, should be on the poor people in our vicinity. There are plenty of them. Whether you yourself are currently frequenting the local soup kitchen or St. Vincent de Paul center or you only drive by such places on the way to work, you know they stay busy. People in your city are in need. They cannot feed their children properly, they can't pay their electric bill, their cars are broken down, they have no job; they are ashamed, demoralized, and ignored. "The poor," said Jesus, "you will always have with you" (Mark 14:7, NAB). That is tragic, but one thing is for sure: you won't run out of opportunities to practice virtue.

Let's narrow it even further, though, to a region that too often escapes our attention: our *immediate* vicinity. Our brothers, our sisters, our mothers, our fathers ... even our in-laws. It is an interesting fact that there are many of us Christ-followers out there who are ready to serve anybody in the human race other than *those* people. But *those* people are the ones God put into our lives. Why do we ignore them? Why, when we serve them and help them (if we do it at all), do we do it in exactly the way our Lord told us not to: with resentment, impatience, and condescension? We can see ourselves bending over some lower-caste wretch from coastal India, ladling water into his mouth. Or if there's someone in need in our own town, let it be someone that we don't really know so that they can give us that wide-eyed look of unalloyed admiration that we value so highly. But family members? Our faces wrinkle up at the thought. *Can't I just send a donation to some destitute Bolivians?*

It is unfortunately true: our least favorite poor people are often the ones we see at Thanksgiving dinner every year.

To help with that natural resentment and irritation we sometimes experience when practicing virtue, we might keep in mind a basic principle: Christians don't serve the poor because they like them — not at first, anyway. They serve them primarily because they love God, and they spy God in the people he made in his image. He loved us first, and gave us the power to love like him. Without him, we "can do nothing" (John 15:5). With him, we bear fruit; we can do anything, and we possess everything. Filled up with his love, we radiate his joy as we serve those he sends our way and, yes, we can even begin to like people we didn't like before. Even relatives.

What Joy Looks Like

What does all this joy look like? Would a person who is joyful be recognizable? Yes, quite often. But a person who is living the fruits of the Holy Spirit is at peace. They are not ostentatious — which is a quality that derives from a lack of peace. So they may very well go unnoticed, just quiet, peaceful people with deep channels of joy flowing beneath their exteriors. You wouldn't realize it until you seriously engaged them, and then it's suddenly revealed. It is kind of shocking.

Not long ago, my wife, Hallie, lobbed four of our children in the car (they were all under the age of eight, so they enjoyed being lobbed) and headed off to meet relatives for a day at the beach. Holding our newborn in my arms, I waved as they backed down the driveway in our sixteen-year-old Saturn with six digits on its odometer and no air conditioning. They were headed across Mobile Bay to the seaside village of Fairhope, a forty-minute drive under a broiling sun. I've never been much of a fan of "summer fun," because in the Deep South that term translates directly into English as "sweat and misery and sunburns and wailing children." That, I'm sure, is why I just *had* to catch up on some work and, unfortunately, couldn't break away — but if they wanted to go without me, I would understand.

Hallie steered the rattling Saturn through Mobile traffic, peering around the rock-shaped gashes in the windshield and negotiating with our middle daughter over the importance of following seatbelt laws. As they neared the exit to Interstate 10, her eyes locked on something completely unexpected.

Though Mobile is a very Catholic town, the exit at Interstate 10 was just another hot, frenzied river of cars and exhaust and pavement and green signs, and as Hallie approached it, she could not help but notice three friars traveling beside the road. In west Mobile, when you say "friar" you pronounce it "frar," and it doesn't suggest anything other than chicken and hot grease. Robed men who have taken vows of poverty, chastity, and obedience don't even enter into the imagination. Hallie, on the other hand, recognized them immediately for what they were.

She had very little time to react, but she experienced an extremely strong impulse to pull up beside them. As a woman, and a shy one at that, with four of her children in the car, she would not ordinarily have considered offering three unknown men a ride, but that's exactly what she found herself doing.

The physical details of the three friars remind me of a fairy tale: there was a short one, a medium-sized one, and a tall one with glasses. They were all beardless and dark-haired. Their grayish blue robes stood out in sharp relief against the rushing interstate traffic. They were of a tiny order called the Little Brothers of the Lamb, a branch of the Dominicans based in France, but they were on their way to help a chapter of the Little *Sisters* of the Lamb build a monastery — in Kansas City. By way of Alabama. They were coming from Texas. I have no explanation for the logic of this route. Regardless, they were extremely pleased to be given a ride across the bay.

They put their enormous backpacks into the trunk and then piled into the Saturn — Saturns are small cars, and it may be that the Holy Spirit did something miraculous with time and space by getting three friars, four kids, and one wife inside at the same time. The friars smelled like sweat, of course, but it wasn't unpleasant. There was too much joy in the air for that to be a problem. As they all headed off down I-10, Hallie was amazed at how joyful they were — more than that, she was caught up in it. More than *that*, what she experienced was the presence of our joyful God right there in the car, lifting all of the occupants up in a spiritual fizz.

They all chattered back and forth — the friars were thrilled by our love of family and faith; Hallie was humbled by their unreserved acceptance of the vocation God had given them. In fact, the littlest one, she said, was silly with happiness; she described him as "a clown for God." The medium-sized one was sweet and deferential; the tall one with glasses was friendly but a little quieter, not being as comfortable with English as the other two. What they had in common, besides the color of their robes, was that their friars' souls were in perfect harmony with the Holy Spirit.

When the Saturn reached the other side of Mobile Bay, Hallie let them off at another exit. She tried to offer them money, but they refused. They accepted only a half-eaten bag of trail mix. Deeply grateful for the assistance, the three friars lined up shoulder-to-shoulder beside the car and sang a triumphal serenade, an ancient hymn, to Hallie and the kids:

> May the Lord bless you and keep you.
> May the Lord make his face to shine upon you
>   and be gracious to you.
> May the Lord lift up his countenance upon you
>   and give you peace.

And off they went, on to Kansas City ... now by way of Florida!

Hallie knew something with exquisite clarity at that point. Though she had only one non-air-conditioned rattletrap car and an out-of-work husband and she had not had a proper haircut in months, she knew that God loved her. He had *shown* her, through a timed explosion of joy shared among herself, her children, and three wandering friars who were unafraid to live the life God had planned for them.

CHAPTER 10

THE EUCHARIST

Forty-five percent of people in the United States who call themselves Catholic think the Eucharist is a fake.[29] In other words, the Church says Holy Communion is the real presence of Jesus — his body, blood, soul, and divinity — but more than four out of ten Church members believe it is only a symbol. "If it's just a symbol," said Flannery O'Connor, "then to hell with it,"[30] and I agree.

It is because it isn't merely symbolic that the Eucharist can't just be something parenthetical or an afterthought, but is in fact "the source and summit of the Christian life" (CCC 1324, LG 11), the Son of God himself, and therefore the burning hot nucleus of all space and time.

There are all kinds of people who just don't believe that, of course. In the above quote, Flannery O'Connor was addressing an entire table of nonbelievers. I myself have a vivid memory of a time that I attempted to explain to a girl I once knew what Catholics believe about the

Eucharist. After I was done she gazed into the distance for a second, then looked back at me and said with unintentionally cartoonish incredulity, "You ... *believe* that?" I don't think I've ever failed to penetrate another person's mind as completely as on that occasion — that is, except for the time not long ago that I attempted to briefly explain the Eucharist to one of my non-Catholic middle school students on the way to the cafeteria at the Catholic school where I once taught. She proceeded to the milk line laughing hysterically at her malformed image of the Host being broken and a bunch of "little Jesuses falling all over the altar."

But then there are the rest of us: the ones who are supposed to believe what the Church teaches about the Eucharist. Do our actions reflect that belief?

Author Mike Aquilina tells a story of a conversation he had with his wife during the early years of their marriage. He was a Catholic; she was a Lutheran. He wanted to explain the Catholic Church's teaching about the Eucharist:

> I pulled down my old *Baltimore Catechism* and read: "After the substance of the bread and wine has been changed into the substance of the body and blood of Our Lord, there remained only the appearances of bread and wine."
>
> "Catholics believe," I explained, "that the real presence means Jesus is there — body, blood, soul and divinity — even after Mass, when the sacrament is reserved in the tabernacle. And there's no longer a crumb we can call bread or a drop we can call wine."

Then that beautiful woman looked up at me from her chair and laughed.

My eyebrows went up. "What's so funny?"

"You don't believe that," she said.

"Yes, I do."

"No, you don't," she replied. "If you do, then why do you only go to Mass on Sunday? You don't even visit the church during the week."

Since that conversation in 1986, I've been to Mass just about every day, and I try not to pass the church without stopping in for a visit to the tabernacle.[31]

Making that kind of quantum leap from what we say we believe about the Eucharist to living that belief is altogether necessary if we're going to seriously embark on a journey to find Christian joy. Jesus is at the heart of the journey. He is both the destination *and* the way we get there.

Without Jesus in the Eucharist, all our sound planning, wise strategies, and good counsel regarding joy will end up on the roadside. It would be like going on a journey without food. Or medicine. Jesus gives us both through this "Most Holy Sacrament." And companionship, too — we need that, as well. When St. Benedict

> Making that kind of quantum leap from what we say we believe about the Eucharist to living that belief is altogether necessary if we're going to seriously embark on a journey to find Christian joy. Jesus is at the heart of the journey.

wrote his famous *Rule* for his monastic order, he specifically excluded the option of being a hermit in service to God. Community is essential.

The Eucharist is all three of these things: food, medicine, and family.

Food

Yes, it tastes like cardboard, but the Eucharist really is food — and not because it has the appearance of a silver-dollar-shaped piece of bread. "For my flesh is true food," Jesus tells a stunned crowd, "and my blood is true drink" (John 6:55, NAB). Jesus insists that he is food for us — *the* Food, in fact: "Unless you eat the flesh of the Son of Man and drink his blood, you do not have life within you" (6:53, NAB). He isn't being metaphorical. The people in the Gospel of John were as scandalized as some people are today, but Jesus offers no qualifications — even when people throw up their hands and walk away in disgust. The Eucharist is a radical new kind of food: Jesus Christ himself, body, blood, soul, and divinity. *Everything* that is essentially Jesus he gives us to consume, to eat, to take into ourselves so that we can be taken into him. The extraordinary life given to us in Baptism would lie weak and listless without it.

Medicine

St. Ignatius of Antioch, writing around A.D. 107, not long after John wrote his Gospel, describes the Eucharist as "the medicine of immortality and the antidote to prevent us from dying."[32] If you were to say that to little children they might not know what you were talking about, but they understand what medicine is: it's what you give them when they are hurting. In the same way, when our souls are hurting from the damage we endure as we live out the Christian life, the medicine we take is Holy Communion. All venial sins are forgiven when we receive; sanctifying grace is strengthened in us; our spiritual life is nourished and fortified. This reality is reinforced at Mass just before Communion, when the priest invites us to the banquet. At that moment, we borrow the words the centurion spoke to Jesus when he sought a healing for his servant[33] and we apply them to ourselves: "Lord, I am not worthy that you should enter under my roof, but only say the word and my soul shall be *healed*." It's medicine.

Family

When we eat ordinary food, we're doing more than just taking objects into our systems and converting them into energy. Food is satisfying on a number of different levels, and one of those levels is the way that it draws us together; that's why dinnertime is so special — we come together and eat as a family, and the food plays a vital role as part of the unification, doesn't it? My dad was so eager to preserve the traditional sanctity of dinnertime (which he never had as a kid) that it was an almost fearful event: dinner was served at six o'clock sharp every night, you didn't come late, and you didn't leave early. Calls might come ringing on the black wall-mounted rotary phone in the kitchen for the entire duration of the meal, but dad refused to acknowledge it or let us acknowledge it, because you *do not answer the phone* during dinnertime. And no singing at the table. Wipe your mouth. Stop choking on that piece of bread.

Good old dad. He was probably overdoing it, but now when I look back, he reminds me of Mr. Banks in *Mary Poppins* ("Kindly do not attempt to cloud the issue with facts!"). At the heart of dinnertime was, and is, something very special: a coming together of people who love each other for the purposes of being renewed in mind, body, and spirit.

That's what the Eucharist does for us, too. Being a Catholic is, above all, being a member of a big, joyful family, the family of God. That is literally true. And when we receive Holy Communion, we are joined more closely to all the people in our family, including all the saints of history whom we've never even met.

Going Back for More

How often should we invite the Lord to enter under our roof? The answer should be obvious. The Church's exact regulations are: once a year, at minimum, preferably during Easter, assuming we are not in a state of mortal sin. But that's the minimum. Even better would be "to receive the holy Eucharist on Sundays and feast days, or more often still, even daily" (CCC 1389). St. Francis de Sales admits it "would be imprudent to advise everyone indiscriminately to receive Communion frequently,"[34] but at the same time he writes: "Go often to Communion … as often as you can with the advice of your spiritual director. And, believe me … by adoring and eating beauty, purity, and goodness itself in this divine sacrament you will become wholly beautiful, wholly good, and wholly pure."[35]

CHAPTER 11

A FAR GREEN COUNTRY

I frequently hear or read the opinions of people who regard heaven the way the characters in George Orwell's *Animal Farm* regard Sugarcandy Mountain: a fairy tale fantasy land promoted by smooth-talking charlatans, a distraction for easily-duped beasts from the all-important task of improving social conditions down here on the farm.

For that kind of person, there is really nothing I can say to encourage them to explore what the Church tells us about heaven. However, no book on Christian joy would be complete without such an exploration. Why? For one thing, it has always been a great comfort to Christians to remember that whatever happens, whatever suffering they have to go through, at the end of it all they'll pass through a door called death and enter an eternal life that will be so wonderful that we can't even imagine it. That's how Paul described it, borrowing from Isaiah: "What no eye has seen, nor ear heard, nor the heart of man conceived, what God has prepared for those who love him" (1 Corinthians 2:9).

That's a beautiful passage. Ironically, it can also have the effect of making heaven the one place we never really talk about. We just repeat, "Well, what no eye has seen, nor ear heard, and all that...." But when do we get there? "Oh, well, no one knows the day or the hour...." The conversation then just sort of evaporates.

In Peter Jackson's *Return of the King*, based on the book by J.R.R. Tolkien, the heroes are trapped in the city while Sauron's forces are snarling and pounding on the gate, about to burst in any minute. The hobbit, Pippin, is in despair because they are all about to die. It is at that moment that Gandalf describes for Pippin, and for us, what happens after we die, using those words that J.R.R. Tolkien in fact put at the end of the book:

> The grey rain-curtain turned all to silver glass and was rolled back, and he beheld white shores and beyond them a far green country under a swift sunrise.

"Well," replies Pippin, noticeably more at ease, "That isn't so bad."

That's how we react as well when, in the midst of all the frustration and death and pain of our lives, we are told this simple truth: those things don't exist in the place we're going.

Time's Up

To take comfort in the notion that heaven is pain-free assumes that we get there, of course. Some of us may not.

Scrooge doesn't *have* to reform his life in *A Christmas Carol*, does he? He could go on ignoring the vision of his name inscribed on the gravestone and keep up his life of materialism and selfishness and wake up in eternity wearing the chains he formed in life, "link by link and yard by yard."[36] But is punishment really a possibility after death, as the Church teaches? What *is* death, anyway? What happens when we die?

For starters, we do not reincarnate. "Human beings die once, and after this the judgment" (Hebrews 9:27, NAB). Belief in reincarnation has increased in past decades, so we should remind ourselves that the Catholic Church teaches against it. Since the truth of her doctrine is guaranteed by the Holy Spirit, we ought to embrace it, however strongly we might feel that we helped Queen Nefertiti design her private gardens or, like General Patton that we personally fought for Carthage in the Punic Wars. We are born and we live one earthly life, and when it's over, it's over.

One way to look at each individual life is to see it "as the time open to either accepting or rejecting the divine grace manifested in Christ" (CCC 1021, cf. 2 Tim 1:9–10). Death is what happens when that allotted time comes to an end. Death often surprises us, but it never surprises God. He knows exactly when you are going to die — whether it is peacefully in a bed at age ninety-three or at twenty-one in a fiery plane crash. God gives the time — it's his alone to give — and he allows it to tick the last tock as he sees fit.

This in no way means we should be fatalists, since God himself encourages us to pray unceasingly and thereby things in this changeable universe can be altered or modified so that even bullets will miss their targets if God chooses — just think of Blessed John Paul II's experience with his would-be assassin. One way or the other, however, God will insist on bringing every lifetime on earth to a close at some point, and only so that he can begin our eternal lives.

When that time comes, the Church teaches that you and I will be judged. There are two perspectives at work when we say "judged."

One is that it is something being done *to us*: God sends his angels to gather us up, he reveals everything about us whether we want him to or not, and he sends some of us to heaven and others off to eternal pain. All of this is important for us to hear so that we can know that nothing we do or think, or any of the repercussions of what we do or think, is hidden from God. He is the absolute ruler of everything, the Pantocrator, and we can no more break off even the smallest piece of his universe and keep it from him than we can swim laps on the surface of the sun.

The second perspective on judgment is that it is something we do *to ourselves*. We see ourselves as we truly are — it will no longer be possible to delude ourselves. We will know and accept that we love God and want to be with him — or we will know and accept that we desire only ourselves. In that sense, we put ourselves in heaven or we willingly choose to be separate from God. We can have it any way we like. Now, *that's* freedom of choice.

It really comes down to love. St. John of the Cross said: "At the evening of life, we shall be judged on our love" (CCC 1022, *Dichos* 64). St. Augustine famously wrote: "My weight is my love,"[37] meaning that we rise to heaven only if we are unencumbered by hatred and selfishness. While love, therefore, equals a type of weightlessness, it *does* have a solid content — it does not mean vague happy thoughts. *How* did we love, in life? *Whom* did we love? Did we love God, the God who has revealed himself? Did we follow his commandments? Or did we follow our own will?

Seeing, At Last

Here's a bizarre concept for you: after we die we will see God "face to face" (1 Corinthians 13:12). That doesn't simply mean we will see the bodily, resurrected Jesus (although we will, of course). It means that the glory of God in his essence will be revealed to us — we will see him face to face. I don't understand how that's possible, but the New Testament promises it and the Church firmly upholds it.

It's true that God is already with us everywhere we go, but we cannot see him with our eyes and we cannot hold him with our arms. The eyes of faith see him just fine — we know he's there. Ultimately, though, what God promises is that in heaven faith will no longer be needed. We will just see him. He will live among us, and "we shall be like him, for we shall see him as he is" (1 John 3:2). The Church calls this the beatific vision, and for all of us it means an "ever-flowing wellspring of happiness, peace, and mutual communion" (CCC 1045).

For the moment "we walk by faith, not by sight" (2 Corinthians 5:7), and the joy we taste is repeatedly lost or pummeled out of us by life in a fractured world. But that mode of living will end in heaven. "I will see you again," says Jesus, "and your hearts will rejoice, and no one will take your joy from you" (John 16:22). That is a promise.

The World We'll Live In

When Jesus chooses to return to earth in glory, every human soul that ever lived will be reunited with its body; it doesn't matter if that body has burnt up, rotted, fallen into a wood chipper, been lost at sea, or disintegrated into atoms. That body will come back to you, where it belongs. It will be resurrected, which means it will not simply come alive again, but will be made to never die again.

God will establish a new heaven and a new earth. My guess is that doesn't mean a new earth as in round mountains instead of conical ones and blue grass instead of green grass, but a radical renewal of everything we are familiar with, as is implied in the *Catechism*: "The visible universe, then, is itself destined to be transformed, 'so that the world itself, restored to its original state, facing no further obstacles, should be at the service of the just,' sharing their glorification in the risen Jesus Christ" (CCC 1047, St. Irenaeus, *Adv. Haeres.* 5, 32,1: PG 7/2, 210).

How Long Will We Be There?

Time, in general, is a tough subject to discuss. What is time? "I know well enough what it is," wrote St. Augustine, "provided that nobody asks me."[38] We live in it and use it and measure it every day, but it tends to defy definitions. That fact only makes it more difficult to discuss timelessness, which is the state of things in heaven.

This is actually a stumbling block for some people who imagine life in heaven as just "going on forever" doing the same set of things. It's frightening — like being trapped on a merry-go-round. Such people can take some solace from the words of Pope Benedict XVI, who assures us that our experience of heaven will be "... not an unending succession of days in the calendar, but something more like the supreme moment of satisfaction, in which totality embraces us and we embrace totality.... We can only attempt to grasp the idea that such a moment is life in the full sense, a plunging ever anew into the vastness of being, in which we are simply overwhelmed with joy."[39]

There is no need to worry that we will get bored in heaven, or run out of things to do, or in any way ever look out across the vastness of eternity and wonder when it will end. We will be too joyful for that.

What Our Bodies Will Be Like

The *Catechism of the Council of Trent* has, for centuries, encouraged priests to tell the faithful about what is waiting for us in heaven according to what has been revealed and what the Church has reasoned out so far.[40]

At the same time, it's important to keep in mind the wise words of a letter written by the Church in 1979: "When dealing with the situation of the human being after death, one must especially beware of arbitrary imaginative

representations."[41] If we engage too frivolously in specu-
lation on post-death existence, we will end up alienating
Christians and non-Christians alike. In short: it's annoying. It makes you sound goofy. People might think your
religion is just a playroom for immature adults.

The letter goes on: "Respect must, however, be given
to the images employed in the Scriptures." Elsewhere, the
letter points out that we can look to the Virgin Mary as
she is now as a model for what we will be like (though to
a lesser degree): "the bodily glorification of the virgin is
an anticipation of the glorification that is the destiny of
all the other elect."[42]

Based on that, and with all soberness, we *can* learn a
few things from the Church about what exactly we have
to look forward to when our eternal lives begin:

- *Subtility*. Remember when Jesus, after the Res-
  urrection, appeared to the disciples in the room
  where they were hiding? He startled them because he just "stood among them" (John 20:19)
  even though the doors were shut and presumably
  locked. That power is what the *Catechism of the
  Council of Trent* calls *subtility*, which is an archaic
  form of *subtlety*, the first definition of which refers to the thinness of fluid or odor. We'll be able
  to achieve a similar quality with our bodies. We
  will no longer be impeded by material objects
  and will be able to pass through them at will —
  just like Jesus.

- *Agility.* No more long, toilsome hikes to reach destinations — if we want to reach the top of a mountain then we'll get there in a flash. Mary demonstrated this power, for instance, at Fatima in 1917 when she appeared from the sky and stood "lightly on the tops of the leaves"[43] of the famous carrasqueira tree where the children first saw her.

- *Brightness.* Our bodies will be beautiful thanks to the purified beauty of our souls, and we will "shine like the sun" (Matthew 13:43). Peter, James, and John saw what that looked like on Mount Tabor during Jesus' Transfiguration.

- *Impassibility.* "They shall hunger no more, neither thirst anymore; the sun shall not strike them, nor any scorching heat" (Revelation 7:16). Nothing will hurt us. Death will be a breezy joke, at most.

About Sex

There will be no sex. Sorry. You might as well come to terms with it.

It makes sense. A fundamental reason for sex is to create babies, but in heaven everyone will already be present to one another — there will be no "later" when someone could be conceived who didn't exist before. Don't fret. The pleasure of sex will not be missed, since it will be superseded by far greater pleasures which sexual pleasure was always meant to foreshadow.

Some of this can be inferred from Jesus' own words in the Gospel of Matthew: "they neither marry nor are given in marriage" in heaven (22:30). Sex, by divine design, is intended expressly for married people (the fact that so many people ignore that intention is irrelevant). If there are no married people in heaven, there is no sex.

Here is another thing about the purpose of marriage and sex: they are for bringing a man and a woman into closer communion with each other and with God. That union is perfectly fulfilled in heaven — marriage and sex will simply lose their point. In the same way that we won't need the gift of faith in heaven because we will see God face-to-face, we will also not need the gifts of sex and marriage, because we will already possess our spouses — and, indeed, everyone one in the community of heaven — perfectly.

> Joy's real source is *spiritual*; it comes from our "heart." God will fix that, too, by taking up permanent residence there, and as a result there will be no envy, or bitterness, or resentment in heaven. You couldn't really have a heaven if those things were still around. Our ordinary state will be joyfulness, like the ones who are already with God now.

Here is what Jesus' words about the absence of marriage *don't* mean: that a man and a woman who were married on earth will no longer have a special relationship in heaven. There is no reason to think that. Yes, the human race will be unified and in harmony with each other, but that doesn't mean everyone will be walking around like smiling zombies acknowledging every single person in exactly the same way — that isn't a heavenly community. That's *Invasion of the Body Snatchers*.

People who were truly special to each other on earth will always be truly special to each other. "Besides the vision of God," wrote Father John Hardon, "heaven means interpersonal relationship among the blessed, and ... ties of blood and friendship begun on earth will somehow continue into eternity."[44]

Food, Glorious Food

In the *Passion of Felicity and Perpetua*, a tale of martyrdom from the early Church, Vibia Perpetua was imprisoned in a Carthaginian dungeon in the year 203 because she wouldn't recant her faith. She asks Jesus to show her a vision that reveals whether she will be released or martyred. She then sees a ladder leading up to heaven with a dragon waiting at the foot of it attempting to keep people from continuing. At the top of the ladder she sees a beautiful garden. Jesus is there. He is completely at peace, and he is milking some sheep — not exactly what you would expect the Son of God, Christ Pantocrator, to be doing. He greets her with a smile and offers her ... *a piece of cheese.*

Altogether the vision confirms that she would, in fact, be martyred, but for our present purposes the point is: there is cheese in heaven.

Perhaps. There is, at any rate, good reason for thinking that we will eat real food with our resurrected bodies, simply because our resurrected Lord ate real food when he appeared to his followers during the forty days before the Ascension. He ate baked fish and bread.

It might seem strange to think that we would need to eat in heaven — won't our hunger and thirst be forever satisfied? But that's just it: we won't *need* to eat, in the sense of having to fill up something that is lacking in our bodies. We will simply enjoy eating. That marvelous rush we get when we bite into a chunk of really fresh cheese will be ours forever (and better, probably).

Rejoicing in Heaven

But now we've come full circle back to those words of Pope Paul VI we discussed in the first chapter. It isn't enough to have piles of external goods like excellent food and wonderful friends and divinized bodies, even in heaven. Joy's real source is *spiritual*; it comes from our "heart." God will fix that, too, by taking up permanent residence there, and as a result there will be no envy, or bitterness, or resentment in heaven. You couldn't really have a heaven if those things were still around. Our ordinary state will be joyfulness, like the ones who are already with God now.

We've been told about them. We know that there is more joy among them over one sinner who repents than over ninety-nine righteous persons who need no repentance (Luke 15:7). The current occupants of heaven don't resent the sinner for taking so long to get his act together, and they don't want to see him raked over hot coals for past misdeeds. They're just glad he's *in* — they're joyful that he's not out in the dark and the cold anymore and is home where he belongs.

Even if we accept that people are like that in heaven, we can't understand how. It can sound suspiciously like entry into heaven will involve a lobotomy or some kind of *A Clockwork Orange*-style brainwashing. It won't, obviously, but then again I have no idea how it is possible that we will be purified of evil inclinations and yet remain *us*, since so much of what we understand about ourselves seems inextricably bound up with our concupiscence, our tendency to sin. On the other hand, I don't understand how a fuel-burning engine runs without blowing up, let alone how it propels a massive shell of metal mounted on wheels down the road with me in it. I just know that it does, and I'm happy to let it.

Presents before Christmas

We have all heard that when it comes to the glorious return of Christ, "no one knows" the appointed hour (Matthew 24:36), and therefore we have to be patient. Interestingly, God does not leave it at that. He is like the father who can't wait for Christmas and lets his kids open a present the day before, just for fun. Although the eternal Christmas — that is, the final revelation of Jesus at the end of time — has not come yet, we have been given a few glimpses.

One of the greatest glimpses of what heaven will actually be like has come to us recently, and from the kind of place that the Lord seems to be very fond of — namely: an unlikely place.

The apparitions of Mary in Rwanda, Africa, have been officially approved by the bishop there, meaning that they are not hoaxes by human beings or deceptions by evil spirits. They are what the Church calls "worthy of veneration." The Church in no way encourages such devotion as being necessary for salvation; however, if the Mother of God takes the time to visit some earthly location with messages for the world, it seems rude (at least; stupid, at worst) to not investigate her appearances.

Beginning in 1981 Mary visited several Rwandan adolescents, referring to herself as "the Mother of the Word." Alphonsine, Anathelie, and Marie-Claire were unrelated to each other by blood, but they all attended the same school in Kibeho, and they all began receiving separate appearances from Mary. Her rapport with the visionaries was very intimate and tender. In fact, many were at first scandalized because the visionaries were so informal with her — they called her "darling" and the equivalent of sweetie-pie; they called her "mama."

Some of the apparitions included an appeal to Rwandans to repent and change their hateful attitudes to each other — a reference to the antagonism between the majority Hutus and the minority Tutsis in Rwanda. The visions could occasionally be terrifying, showing in graphic detail what would eventually happen in 1994: the genocide that left over a million Rwandans dead, hacked apart and literally clogging the rivers. It was not presented as a punishment, but as the natural, logical consequence of people's deep, sustained hatred toward each other. Mary wants to save her children from that fate. The visionaries were also taken by Mary on supernatural tours — while their bodies remained in a kind of comatose state their souls saw heaven, purgatory, and hell. The things they saw defied all that they understood about reality. According to Anathelie, the inhabitants of heaven played music without instruments — their various "sensation[s] of contentment and joy"[45] produced the melodies. There were many different worlds available to visit, including one made entirely of "vivid color and light, and people traveled from place to place by sliding through the light."[46] A fourth visionary, Vestine, accompanied Jesus himself on an excursion through heaven, and had this to say:

> There were colors I'd never seen before and they sounded like music, and music like I'd never heard before that sounded like color. There are no words.... I don't know how to explain the feeling of being there because I've never felt anything like it. [47]

In Exultation

All this is where we're going. It's our destiny. No hatred, no wars, no suffering, no boredom or stupidity, no frustration or sorrow. A new heaven and a new earth, an expansive way of living where in total freedom we will enjoy the endless gifts of God without ever having to worry that they will run out. Most of all, we will have God himself, without any obstacles between him and us. We will see him, and know him, and know that all the joy we've ever known was him, and all the joy we could ever experience is him, and that "no one will take your joy from you" (John 16:22).

Getting there requires abandoning our will to his will and enduring with love whatever comes our way. That includes suffering, poverty, and death. Those are horrible things, and Jesus is not being flippant about them when he assures us that they will be forgotten ultimately, the way labor pains are forgotten by a mother after her baby is born. We just have to persevere.

> In this you rejoice, though now for a little while you may have to suffer various trials, so that the genuineness of your faith, more precious than gold which though perishable is tested by fire, may redound to praise and glory and honor at the revelation of Jesus Christ. Without having seen him you love him; though you do not now see him you believe in him and rejoice with unutterable and exalted joy. (1 Peter 1:6–8)

EPILOGUE

My dad died before this book could be published. I had been looking forward to the moment when I would hand him a copy and see on his face that shimmery paternal pride which most every son cherishes, but I guess that moment was not meant to be.

He was seventy-five years old. His body had been the beneficiary of medical marvels his ancestors could only have dreamed of and without which it would have long before given up its ghost. In particular, he'd had another man's heart in his chest for the last fifteen years; the work once done by his now withered kidneys was performed by a home dialysis machine. Insulin injections controlled his diabetes. Lortab helped with the pain.

Just helped, though. Dad was in constant pain well before the end. It hammered against his atrophied muscles and in his joints and upon the innumerable breaches where brittle skin had torn or where little cancerous tumors had been removed. Pain had practically become a part of his body, like a new limb. But he also knew what pain *was*, in its most abstract sense, and why it was best described as a cross — and he understood what he was supposed to do with it, and not do with it. You didn't whine about the cross, you didn't cry about it, you didn't wish it away. You picked it the hell up and walked with it to whichever barren hill God wanted and you planted it firmly in the ground. That was my dad. Back in 2005 he had watched Pope John Paul II carry *his* cross right up to the end, and now it was time to carry his own.

At the same time, the man who understood the reality of the cross was the same man who had the experience I described in Chapter 1. He had tasted transcendental joy in the hush of St. Joseph's, he had drunk it in and breathed it; his soul saw it. True to his word, he never forgot it. But memory has different depths — there are those memories that live and move in us, connecting us to a moment as genuinely as our eyes connect us to the present. Other memories become like messages to ourselves, scribbled on old, carefully preserved note paper and kept under glass in an interior museum. We acknowledge them, but we can't be moved by them the way we were moved on the day they were written. Dad's experience of joy back in 1968 was like one of those preserved notes. It had no power left to drive away the teeth-grinding pain that gnawed at his body in the final weeks of his life.

When paramedics brought him to the hospital (Dad despised hospitals, the way a good Pole despises Nazism or a child despises green peas), his organs were shutting down; his body was in a state of septic shock. He could maintain consciousness only for brief periods, and would fall asleep in the middle of sentences. He told my older brother, David: "Dave, I don't think I'm going to make it this time" — unexpected words from a man who traditionally guarded his place in the world with extreme prejudice. In his hospital room, he was overcome by anxiety, even anger, as if he was desperate to survive, to break out and return to the world. That was Monday.

By Tuesday he had fallen into something like a comatose state. His body was saturated with infection, though doctors were purportedly getting it under control, if only in the same way a person has control over a fistful of warm mud. Everyone in my family was having the conversations that needed to be had, thick-skinned geometrical conversations about getting ready, being prepared, and acknowledging reality. My mom took some time to go home and shower. She tried eating, but stress had stolen her appetite weeks before. She was down to about a hundred pounds.

On Friday, Dad woke up. In fact, he almost leapt up. My oldest brother Mike was there. So was Susan, in the black and white of her order, with special permission by her Mother Superior. Dad woke up and bathed them both in the invisible light of a startling ebullience. He was talking loudly — from emotion, they thought at first, until everyone realized he had gone as deaf as a post. When mom, at that moment, happened to appear in the doorway, Dad spied her and shouted, "Darling! My darling!" She hurried to him, and he kissed her, and he laughed, and she laughed. As always, she scooted around him looking for ways to make him more comfortable or to soothe him, but he just didn't need it. "You are so cute!" he said, and he meant it probably more deeply than he'd ever meant it. He felt no pain in his body, and so for the time being his doctor saw no reason to give him pain medication.

Very soon a steady stream of correspondence began between my newly deaf dad and everyone else; on paper it was explained that he had been unconscious for three days, that his body was failing and infected, and that there were no real solutions to any of it.

Dad, however, was now unconcerned with diagnoses. He had gained possession of a certainty that his time on earth was very limited. And he was ready.

His blue eyes blazed, and he said what I now realize was exactly what my sister Susan said years ago in the flowerbeds with her knee torn beneath her, unable to stand and sweat running along the lines of an unconquerable smile: "It's worth it." He had endured so much suffering, and he felt sure that the suffering would return soon. "No matter what happens," my dad assured us, "this is worth it."

Wherever he'd gone during his coma, he had returned filled with this profound joy. He was not simply trying to cheer everyone up or put on a brave face — what he felt was from the roots of his guts, and he knew that God had put it there. It was that second fruit of the Holy Spirit, the fruit of a life lived in obedience to God's law, the fruit of suffering given as a gift to the suffering Christ. It was also, it seems to me, a glowing coat of sealant put upon the hulls of a ship before a voyage.

On Monday, the pain did begin to come back. The joyousness passed gently like a spring rain, and mom could see that he was hurting again. He wouldn't admit it,

Wherever he'd gone during his coma, he had returned filled with this profound joy. He was not simply trying to cheer everyone up or put on a brave face — what he felt was from the roots of his guts, and he knew that God had put it there. It was that second fruit of the Holy Spirit, the fruit of a life lived in obedience to God's law, the fruit of suffering given as a gift to the suffering Christ.

though, because he didn't want her to worry. His hearing returned, much to everyone's amusement. Mom asked him if he was sad. "Oh, no. I'm not sad." He meant it.

On Tuesday, he died. The family gathered together as they should, as they must, and I observed in others the entire range of human emotion flowing and churning like waves on a river. There was sadness, of course; some anger; some disorientation. For me, I must confess, there was mostly just happiness and pride. Happiness for him; that he had made it, he had run the race and passed into everlasting joy (assisted by many, many prayers and mass intentions, doubtless); pride that he had faced his trials bravely, intentionally, like John Paul II.

And I am happy because I have an example to emulate — that's why I offer it here, as well, for the benefit of others. The fruit of joy doesn't necessarily bloom according to easily recognizable schedules, still less when we think we'd like it to. But it's growing, even in darkness and suffering. Especially in darkness and suffering. It's in us, because the Holy Spirit is in us, and he never gives up on us. We should never give up on him. It's worth it.

NOTES

1 Madrid, Patrick, "The Prophet of Hyde Park," *Crisis Magazine*, March 2002, 30–35.

2 *Summa Theologica*, I, II, q. 70, article 3.

3 Leen, Edward, *The Holy Spirit and His Work in Souls* (New York, NY: Scepter, 2008), 216.

4 Ibid., 183.

5 Kreeft, Peter. "How to Win the Culture War," *The Integrated Catholic Life*, June 16, 2010. http://www.integratedcatholiclife.org/2010/06/kreeft-how-to-win-the-culture-war/.

6 From *Gaudium et Spes*: "Although he was made by God in a state of holiness, from the very onset of his history man abused his liberty, at the urging of the Evil One. Man set himself against God and sought to attain his goal apart from God" (13).

7 Tom Hoopes, "The Dark Backward: Demons in the Real World." *Crisis*, Nov. 2003, 14–20.

8 All quotes from St. Thomas used in this chapter are from *Summa Theologica*. I,II, q. 70, article 3, www.newadvent.org.

9 St. Francis de Sales, *Introduction to the Devout Life* (New York: Doubleday, 2003), Part 3, # 10.

10 Flannery, Austin, ed., *Vatican Council II: The Conciliar and Post Conciliar Documents, New Revised Edition* (New York: Costello, 1992), 34.

11 See John Paul II, *Laborem Exercens*, 5–6, www.vatican.va.

12 Pope Benedict XVI, *General Audience*, given Wednesday, August 3, 2011. www.vatican.va.

13 Pope John Paul II, *Laborem Exercens*, 6.6.

14 Rutler, George. *St John Vianney: The Curé d'Ars Today*. San Francisco: Ignatius, 1988.

15 Ibid.

16 Chesterton, G.K. *Saint Francis of Assisi* (New York: Doubleday, 1990), 56.

17 St. Maria Faustina Kowalska, *Diary* (Stockbridge, MA; Marians of the Immaculate Conception, 2002), 118.

18 Ibid., 229.

19 Cf. http://www.jewishvirtu allibrary.org/jsource/biogra phy/Kolbe.html.

20 All references in this section are from the NAB translation of 1 Maccabees.

21 Kreeft, Peter, ed. *Summa of the Summa* (San Francisco: Ignatius Press, 1990), 106.

22 Edith Stein, *The Hidden Life: Essays, Meditations, Spiritual Texts*, L. Gelber and Michael Linssen, eds., Waltraut Stein, trans.(Washington, D.C.: ICS 1996), 92.

23 Bolt, Robert, *A Man for All Seasons* (New York: Scholastic Book Services, 1967), 73.

24 Stein, *The Hidden Life*, 93.

25 Ciszek, Walter J., *He Leadeth Me* (San Francisco: Ignatius, 1995), 49.

26 Ibid., 77–78, emphasis added.

27 St. Francis de Sales, *Finding God's Will for You* (Manchester: Sophia Institute Press, 1998), 52, 56, 60, 63.

28 http://www.npr. org/2011/07/09/137348637/ in-uganda-american- becomes-foster-mom-to- 13-girls.

29 http://www.pewforum. org/U-S-Religious- Knowledge-Survey-Who- Knows-What-About-Reli gion.aspx#Christianity.

30 O'Connor, Flannery, *The Habit of Being*. Letters edited and with an introduction by Sally Fitzgerald (New York: Farrar, Straus, & Giroux, 1979), "To 'A,'" July 5, 1958: 290–91.

31 Aquilina, Mike, *Love in the Little Things: Tales of Family Life* (Cincinnati: Servant, 2007), 13–14.

32 *Letter to the Ephesians*, XX, www.newadvent.org.

33 Matthew 8:8, NAB.

34 *Introduction to the Devout Life*, II, 20.

35 Ibid., II, 21.

36 Dickens, Charles, *A Christmas Carol* (B & N Classics: New York, 2004), 23.

37 St. Augustine, *Confessions* (New York: Barnes and Noble Books, 1992), 317.

38 Ibid., 14.

39 *Spe Salvi*, 12, www.vatican .va.

40 XI, XII.

41 Jacquis Dupuis, ed., *The Christian Faith in the Doctrinal Documents of the Catholic Church* (New York: Alba House, 2001), 1027. *Letter of the Sacred Congregation for the Doctrine of the*

Faith on Certain Questions Concerning Eschatology, 7.

42 Ibid., 1027.

43 Pelletier, Joseph A., *The Sun Danced at Fatima* (New York: Image, 1983), 27.

44 Hardon, John, *The Catholic Catechism* (New York: Image, 1981), 267.

45 Ilibagiza, Immaculée, *Our Lady of Kibeho* (Carlsbad: Hay House, 2008), 136.

46 Ibid., 136.

47 Ibid., 142–143.

BIBLIOGRAPHY

2011 Our Sunday Visitor's Catholic Almanac. Huntington: Our Sunday Visitor, 2011. Ed. Matthew Bunson, D. Min.

Aquilina, Mike. *Love in the Little Things: Tales of Family Life.* Cincinnati: Servant, 2007.

Bolt, Robert. *A Man for All Seasons.* New York: SBS, 1967.

Catechism of the Catholic Church. New York: Image, 1995.

Chesterton, G.K. *Saint Francis of Assisi.* New York: Image, 1990.

Chesterton, G.K. *Saint Thomas Aquinas.* New York: Image, 1990.

Ciszek, Walter J. *He Leadeth Me.* San Francisco: Ignatius, 1995.

Daniélou, Jean. *The Bible and the Liturgy.* Notre Dame: University of Notre Dame Press, 1956.

Dickens, Charles. *A Christmas Carol.* B & N Classics: New York, 2004.

Durant, Will. *Age of Faith.* New York: MJF, 1950.

Fellowship of Catholic Scholars Newsletter, Volume 8, Number 4. http://www.catholicscholars.org/publications/quarterly/v8n4sep1985.pdf.

Gard, Richard, Ed. *Buddhism.* George Braziller, 1962.

Giorgi, Rosa. *Saints: A Year in Faith and Art.* New York: Abrams, 2005.

Hardon, John. *The Catholic Catechism.* New York: Image, 1981.

Hardon, John. *Pocket Catholic Dictionary.* New York: Image, 1985.

Hero of Auschwitz. Libertyville: Marytown Press, 2002.

Hoopes, Tom. "The Dark Backward: Demons in the Real World." *Crisis,* Nov. 2003, 14–20.

Ignatius Catholic Study Bible, 2nd Edition. San Francisco: Ignatius, 2010.

Ilibagiza, Immaculée. *Our Lady of Kibeho.* Carlsbad: Hay House, 2008.

Introduction to St. Thomas Aquinas. New York: Random House, 1948. Ed. Anton C. Pegis.

Kreeft, Peter, ed. *Summa of the Summa.* San Francisco: Ignatius Press, 1990.

Kreeft, Peter, and Ronald K. Tacelli. *Handbook of Christian Apologetics.* Downers Grove: InterVarsity Press, 1994.

Leen, Edward. *The Holy Spirit and His Work in Souls.* New York: Scepter, 2008.

Madrid, Patrick. "The Prophet of Hyde Park." *Crisis Magazine* (March 2002): 30–35.

O'Connor, Flannery, *The Habit of Being.* Letters edited and with an introduction by Sally Fitzgerald (New York: Farrar, Straus, & Giroux, 1979), To "A," July 5, 1958: 290–291

Orwell, George. *Animal Farm.* New York: Signet, 1946.

Passion of Felicity and Perpetua. Medieval Sourcebook. http://www.fordham.edu/halsall/source/perpetua.html.

Pelletier, Joseph A. *The Sun Danced at Fatima.* New York: Image, 1983.

Pope Benedict XVI. *Sacramentum Caritatis.* Boston: Pauline, 2007.

Pope Benedict XVI. *Deus Caritas Est.* Vatican City: Libreria Editrice Vaticana, 2006.

Pope Benedict XVI. *Spe Salvi.* http://www.vatican.va/holy_father/benedict_xvi/encyclicals/documents/hf_ben-xvi_enc_20071130_spe-salvi_en.html.

Pope Benedict XVI. *Caritas in Veritate.* http://www.vatican.va/holy_father/benedict_xvi/encyclicals/documents/hf_ben-xvi_enc_20090629_caritas-in-veritate_en.html.

Pope Benedict XVI. *Jesus of Nazareth, Part II.* San Francisco: Ignatius, 2011.

Pope Benedict XVI, *General Audience,* given Wednesday, August 3rd, 2011. http://www.vatican.va/holy_father/benedict_xvi/

audiences/2011/documents/hf_ben-xvi_aud_20110803_en.html.

Pope John Paul II. *Laborem Exercens*. Boston: Pauline, 1981.

Pope Paul VI. *Gaudete in Domino.* http://www.vatican.va/holy_father/paul_vi/apost_exhortations/documents/hf_p-vi_exh_19750509_gaudete-in-domino_en.html.

Ratzinger, Joseph. *The Ratzinger Report*. San Francisco: Ignatius, 1985.

Rutler, George. *St. John Vianney: The Curé d'Ars Today*. San Francisco: Ignatius, 1988.

Sheed, Frank. *Theology and Sanity*. New York: Sheed and Ward, 1946.

St. Augustine. *Confessions*. New York: Barnes and Noble, 1992.

St. Augustine. *City of God*. New York: Image, 1958.

St. Francis de Sales. *Finding God's Will for You*. Manchester: Sophia Institute Press, 1998.

St. Francis de Sales. *Introduction to the Devout Life*. New York: Image, 2003. Ed. John K. Ryan.

St. Maria Faustina Kowalska. *Diary: Divine Mercy in My Soul*. Stockbridge: Marians of the Immaculate Conception, 2002.

Stein, Edith. *The Hidden Life: Essays, Meditations, Spiritual Texts*, L. Gelber and Michael Linssen, eds., Waltraut Stein, trans. (Washington, D.C.: ICS 1996).

Summa Theologica. New Advent. http://www.newadvent.org/summa/.

The Basic Sixteen Documents of Vatican Council II. Northport: Costello, 1996. Ed. Austin Flannery, O.P.

The Catechism of the Council of Trent. Rockford: Tan, 1982.

The Catholic Study Bible. Oxford: Oxford University Press, 2006. Ed. Donald Senior, John J. Collins.

The Christian Faith in the Doctrinal Documents of the Catholic Church. New York: Alba House, 2001. Ed. Jacques Dupuis.

The Early Church Fathers on CD-ROM. Salem: Harmony Media, Inc., 2000.

The Encyclicals of John Paul II. Huntington: Our Sunday Visitor, 2001. Ed. J. Michael Miller, C.S.B.

The New Jerome Biblical Commentary. Upper Saddle River: Prentice Hall, 1990. Ed. Raymond Brown, S.S., Joseph A. Fitzmyer, S.J., Roland E. Murphy, O.Carm.

The Pocket Aquinas. New York: Simon and Schuster, 1960. Ed. Vernon J. Bourke.

The Summa Theologica of St. Thomas Aquinas, Vol. II. Allen: Christian Classics, 1981.

Tolkien, J.R.R. *The Return of the King.* New York: Houghton Mifflin, 2002.

Voltaire. *Candide.* New York: Bantam, 1959.

William Shakespeare: The Complete Works. Oxford: Clarendon, 1998. Ed. Stanley Wells, Gary Taylor, John Jowett, and William Montgomery.